IDENTITY CRISIS

(A LAWYER'S TALE):

HOW DIVORCE NEARLY ENDED MY LIFE

ROBERT L. WEGMAN ESQ

TABLE OF CONTENTS

Identity Crisis (A Lawyer's Tale): How Divorce Nearly Ended My Life

© 2024 by Robert L. Wegman

Published in Hampton, VA, by Fruition Publishing Concierge Services®. Fruition Publishing Concierge Services® is a division of Alesha Brown, LLC.

Fruition Publishing Concierge Services® can bring authors to your live event. For more information or to book an event, visit Fruition Publishing Concierge Services® at

www.FruitionPublishing.com

ISBN: 978-1-954486-50-8 Paperback

ISBN: 978-1-954486-51-5 eBook

Library of Congress Control Number: 2024915657

Unless otherwise noted, all scriptures are from The Holy Bible, King James Version. (1979). Cambridge Edition.

FRUITION
PUBLISHING
CONCIERGE SERVICES®

FRUITIONPUBLISHING.COM

A DIVISION OF ALESHA BROWN, LLC

DEDICATIONS

I dedicate this book to the following people:

∼

First, *to my brother, Scott Edward Wegman (October 15, 1969 - October 7, 1988). Scott, your life touched me in profound ways I am only now beginning to grasp. I would endure all the anguish of this past year over again if I could have you back for 30 minutes, but I know we will meet again someday. Thank you for saving my life.*

∼

Second, to my children, Rob and Danielle Wegman. You are truly the loves of my life and without your steadfast love and support, I would not have weathered this storm. Thank you!

∾

Third, to the handful of diehard people who were instrumental not only in assisting me with this book, but more importantly, assisting me with life:

Ady Shea, my counselor, for believing in me and validating my feelings.

Mara Rosen, for your thoughtful critiques of my manuscripts.

Kelli Tyler, for answering my desperate calls at all hours of the night, and for your food that was always prepared with love.

and most important

Judyth Mawyin, for loving me when I needed it the most.

INTRODUCTION

Trigger Warning:

This book contains sensitive content that may be distressing to some readers. It addresses topics such as divorce, emotional distress, mental health struggles, and suicidal thoughts. Readers who may be affected by these themes are advised to proceed with caution and seek support if needed.

Have you ever wondered what causes people to take their own lives? What goes through their minds moments before they make that fateful decision? Sadly, I came close to knowing. I was paralyzed with massive, burning anxiety and my thoughts took me to a perilous place where I thought I was losing my mind. The anxiety was so overwhelming that I contemplated taking my life.

I realize now that what I experienced for nearly a year was overwhelming anxiety and hopelessness that interfered with my mind's ability to process information and understand the differences between truth and reality. I was overwhelmed, distraught, and depressed.

Suicidal thoughts were prevalent, and I literally had to talk my way out of them often. Had it not been for my faith, a few healthy synapses in my brain, and a handful of friends, I would have ended my life. As I wrote this book, I became increasingly grateful that God spared my life. For reasons I may never fully understand, He has another plan for me. I must not squander this golden opportunity to live my best life. I also want to share my story, hoping that perhaps I can help a few others.

Although this book is about my life and my struggles—some of which are still ongoing—my life, *per se,* is not the compelling part of this story. I hope that my life and this book can be used as a springboard for further discussions about mental health. We can and must do better to help each other.

We can continue to bury our heads in our smart-phones and communicate through social media and text messages or we can get back to basics and begin loving, calling, and caring for our fellow humans once again. For those who are avid texters, calling someone may seem outdated, but texts are lifeless and cold. We attach emojis to them to provide some life and warmth, but they are still usually cold, and can lead to confusion and misunderstandings. Text messages are devoid of life because they lack true emotion. People will often text things they would never say in person or over the telephone where they are held accountable in real time. Text messages are convenient and they have their place, but there is no substitute for the sound, inflection, and passion of another person's voice.

If I achieved nothing else through my writing, I hope I have at least provided a framework for others to follow or avoid when faced with a similar crisis of identity or mental health issue. I fully recognize that there is no one-size-fits-all approach, and that what worked for me may not work for others, but I hope this book will provide a message of hope for those who have lost their identity because of death, retirement, divorce, unemployment, and so forth.

Whenever I complained about my life, my ex-mother-in-law always reminded me that the first hundred years are the hardest. I have often repeated that line and it has always gotten a laugh, but she was so right. Life is hard. It gets messy and divorce can be even messier. Life does not always go according to plan, and we must accept that reality. We must equally accept that we have only one life and choose to withdraw from the things that make us uneasy, or forge ahead and conquer our fears.

One of my lodestars is retired North Carolina State University head basketball coach, Jim Valvano. Coach V, as he is known, delivered an incredibly motivational speech during the ESPY Awards on March 3, 1993, after receiving the Arthur Ashe Award. He gave his speech a mere two months prior to his passing from cancer, which is likely why he was assisted onto the stage. Although the entire speech is motivational and inspirational and definitely worth watching in its entirety, the most memorable line is simple but powerful: *Never give up; never, ever give up.*

I am confident that Coach V never gave up until his dying breath. His advice is so relevant and, although clinging to life while your world spirals out of control is easier said than done, it can be done. I am living proof of that. I encourage you also to seek whatever help you need, professional or otherwise, to not only stay alive but to thrive.

CHAPTER 1

IDENTIFYING THE CRISIS

My downward spiral, and the loss of my identity, begin in July 2021 when my wife messaged me about her return from visiting her family in New York. She was coming home, but only to gather a few things and leave for good.

I always knew our marriage was on shaky footing, but my wife and I were good friends. We had longevity on our side—thirty-one years, to be exact—and we communicated well. We traveled together, laughed together, and had children together. I suppose I should have seen her departure as inevitable, but I was in denial. Afterward, I was left to reconstruct my life on my own. That is when, at age sixty, my life derailed.

My story is not unique. Statistically, half of all marriages in the United States end in divorce. Perhaps it sounds trite, but anyone who knows me will tell you my family was my life and identity. The two were inextricably intertwined. My role as head of my household, principal bread winner, patriarch, and mentor to many down-trodden clients was my raison d'être (reason to live). Every decision I ever made, save a few reckless ones, was made only after considering what was in the best interests of my family.

I strongly suspect that my journey is like those endured by many others—even those who ended their lives and are unable to tell their stories. Perhaps some will read this and question why I struggled at all. I was financially secure, had a good job, and was living in the marital home. Many have far fewer material and financial resources than I, but during this year-long test, none of this seemed to matter. I all but gave up.

I suppose one way of thinking about this is to compare two people: one with means and one without. If the first has a net worth of one million dollars and the other one thousand, and each goes bankrupt, they end up in roughly the same financial place. Their individual struggles are real regardless of where they started. My money, assets, and even my station in life were irrelevant to me. The crisis itself became all-encompassing and consumed nearly all the free space in my mind. I obsessed over everything, leaving little room for any other thoughts.

Almost everyone—whether rich or poor, funny and outgoing, introverted and shy, mentally tough or chronically struggling—has felt despair. Many have been driven to commit suicide: an act that ends their physical and mental suffering but causes additional suffering for those who remain behind.

My life became a paradox. I had a crisis that needed to be fixed and I felt damned if I did anything to fix, and even more damned if I did nothing.

I have heard many say that suicide is a selfish act because those who choose that option ostensibly fail to consider its effects on those left behind. I suspect nothing could be further from the truth. The pain and anguish I felt were palpable. They were excruciating, and I could think of nothing else that might work to stop them. I thought of those who would be left behind, particularly my children, but they were competing with that formidable voice in my head that kept telling me to end my suffering.

Had I committed suicide, those left behind would have undoubtedly performed a post-mortem examination to figure out why I ended my life without considering anyone else. I suspect they would have questioned whether signs were apparent and overlooked, even though the signs were obvious.

Because I have been exposed to many suicide cases, I know people often think about how the person's permanent and myopic solution affects their legacy. From the moment of one's death by suicide, nothing else about his or her life matters. He would forever be remembered not as a good father or for his good and charitable deeds, but only as the person who committed suicide and thought of no one else. But this conclusion is fraught with hypocrisy and selfishness.

People must understand the decision to take one's own life is very often not a split-second decision. Sure, people can snap and commit extreme acts like suicide and homicide, but in my case, it was a gradual building process that brought me to that point. Suicide would have been the final act, the coup de grâce.

Ironically, those capable of intervening to save a life sometimes later support the cause by joining suicide prevention groups. This participation might alleviate their guilt or enhance their reputation as empathetic individuals. Yet these *victims* are often the very people who willfully or negligently ignore people in crisis.

People make excuses for not intervening, but the truth is we (myself included) are self-centered and prioritize our well-being over others. Most people are fundamentally ignorant about suicide until it is too late, at which point their sympathies mean nothing. Regrettably, I can count on one hand the people who were concerned enough to check on me from time to time.

The truth sometimes hurts, but the truth is the truth. I know because I endured a year-long struggle where my family members, colleagues, so-called friends, and even professional organizations, whose sole charter is to assist people in crisis, didn't care enough to help me.

Although some people may have been well-intentioned, few really understood that when a crisis occurs, time is of the essence. A crisis cannot wait for one week or even one day. One cannot check on a person when they return from a vacation or a business conference. It will probably be too late. Predictably, when a death by suicide occurs, people alter their plans, vacations, conferences and the like to bid farewell to the departed. Yet we will not cancel those same commitments to help a person in crisis. I say this not as a matter of condemnation but as a cold, hard fact.

To be fair, people sometimes do not know what to do or say to people who are manic or in the throes of full-blown anxiety and depression. And to be even more fair, people have their own lives and issues (e.g., mental, financial, interpersonal) and find it difficult to assume someone else's problems. But the little things—a mere phone call, a meal, physical presence, a little guidance, and an occasional wellness check—are reassuring and can remind a depressed person that others care. Those simple actions can be instrumental in quieting the voices that urge someone to end their life.

In my case, I must lay some of the blame at my own feet. Whenever I am experiencing a hard time, I tend to withdraw from everyone and everything I know. I fail to reach out for help, not out of some sense of embarrassment or shame, but because I refuse to be a burden on anyone. Retrospectively, I had either intentionally or unwittingly constructed a metaphorical Potemkin village to disguise my innermost feelings. Simplistically, I was following the philosophy of *fake it 'til you make it.*

However, neighbors, friends, and family all knew what I was going through and, though they may not have had time to take on my life as a full-time project, a short phone call would have been well-received, much appreciated, and potentially life-saving.

I happen to be blessed with a strong mental fortitude. I am able to talk myself out of bad and perilous situations, but not without paying a hefty price. As mentally tough as I think I am, I found myself engaged in negotiations with myself about the costs and benefits of suicide. I ignored the obvious conflict of interest and began, in effect, bargaining for and against my life.

CHAPTER 2
A WONDERFUL LIFE

I am no expert on depression, anxiety, crises, or suicide causes and effects, nor do I care to be. I only know had I continued down the path on which I was headed, it would not have been a split-second decision. Suicide would have resulted from great suffering where I saw no path to happiness.

Like George Bailey in *It's A Wonderful Life*, I spent most of my life caring for others with verifiably stellar results and yet in the throes of my burning anxiety. I felt the world would be better off without me. I wished I had never been born. Also, like George, I did not want to burden my family or friends, so I felt very alone in dealing with my problems.

What I realize now is the remedy for anxiety and depression is to have *good* people around you who listen without trying to solve your problems or compare their lives to yours. You need people who know how to listen, not fix, but listen. People who will not compare their lives with yours but listen and ONLY listen. Listening seems easy enough, but few can resist the temptation to provide anecdotes about their own lives or regale you with stories of how great their lives are while you are wondering how to survive the next day.

The feelings I had were real not just to me but objectively to my therapist, who validated my feelings. The factual underpinnings for those feelings may not have been based entirely on truth or fact, but in my mind's eye, they were rooted in both. I thought no one cared about me, so any harm caused by my death would be de minimis and fleeting at best. My life came down to one simple question: who really cared if I lived or died?

I often fancifully thought if only my life could be like George Bailey's—where his friends and family rallied to his side and showered him with love, adoration, and money—all my problems would be solved. George was a good man—a man who put others ahead of himself, but because of a twist of fate, he believed the world would have been better off if he was never born. Why did he feel that way? Stress. His uncle accidentally gave away all the bank's daily proceeds, leaving George $8,000 short, just as the bank examiner was about to perform an audit. George had no discernible mental illness. In an instant, he simply felt overwhelmed and unable to cope with the rigors of life and the situation in which he found himself.

But George had a guardian angel who saved his life and helped him to recognize his life had value and impact. Unfortunately, guardian angels are not as obvious or committed as Clarence Odbody—the quirky guardian angel who rescued George Bailey —but they exist. Sometimes, people find them in the oddest of places. In my case, my guardian angels worked as a grocery store cashier and as a dry cleaner. My principal guardian angel was a woman from Ecuador and her wonderful family who took the time to love me when I felt I was unlovable.

Make no mistake, guardian angels are out there, but you must seek them. Sometimes they seek us and if we are receptive and willing to believe in the goodness of our fellow man, we will know when we see them. But for as much as guardian angels exist, I must caution you, evil spirits do too. Regrettably, those spirits will revel in your unfortunate plight or worse, actively seek to undermine anything positive you have in your life.

Case in point: Upon turning fifty, I decided to reward my hard work and success with a BMW 528i. I wanted a BMW since my days in college, where I spent time in Germany with my then-girlfriend, a German foreign exchange student. Her father drove a 5-series BMW and after hearing that engine purr at speeds of 225 kilometers per hour (140 miles per hour) on the German autobahn, I knew I needed to get one before I died. A BMW to me truly was the ultimate driving machine.

Yet, once I finally leased one, I found that every other month or so I had to replace at least one run-flat tire because someone had stuck a nail in its sidewall, rendering it useless and not fixable. I had to buy a new tire every time at around $400.00 a tire. It became obvious to me I was being sabotaged. Someone could not bear that I had something symbolizing success and wealth, and seemed to take the position that if he could not have it neither should I. I bring this up because as important as it is to recognize that good people in your life exist, negative forces of jealousy and resentment are equally prevalent.

We as Americans love a good rags-to-riches and comeback story and most will cheer you on and revel in your success. Conversely and regrettably, society is also filled with people who will figuratively stick a nail in your sidewall at their first opportunity. Despite that, I think country singer Luke Bryan has it right when he says most people are good in his song of the same name. Though I agree with this sentiment, I also recognize an important key to life is discernment. Seek those who lift you up and release those who wish to tear you down. It is *your* life, and you only get one for a brief period. Make the most of it.

Though this book is about my divorce and stages of grief, sadly, millions worldwide share similar stories. Many have experienced the same, similar, or even worse, setbacks in life. Some readers may even wonder how a man who seemingly had it all could find himself in any sort of crisis. After all, outwardly I was educated, successful, respected, loved, and revered by many. I owned three houses and a boat—things many people never acquire in a lifetime. But none of these things mattered. I have often told people I doubt anyone lying on his deathbed says *I am going to miss my vacation house.* In fact, in many respects, this collection of assets made severing ties with my spouse far more complicated.

I saw my life and things I built through my blood, sweat, tears, and sacrifice systematically dismantled and nothing I could do would alter that course. My new reality was coming whether I liked it or not, and I was unprepared to stop the destructive forces headed my way. There was no cone of uncertainty; the massive negative forces were locked onto me like a Sidewinder Missile to its target. I felt my life going down in flames and I could only hold on and literally pray I survived the aftermath. If that sounds melodramatic, I can assure you it is not. I have neither the vocabulary nor the literary mastery to describe the sickening feeling of staring at a bottle of pills while engaging in an internal struggle over whether to down them all at once to end my life.

Colleagues of mine asked why I did not seek counseling if I was struggling so much as if counseling was the panacea for all I was going through. Candidly, I can only attribute it to one thing—hubris. I had always been the fixer—the guy who helped others get out of problems. I was a criminal defense attorney. I knew it all and had seen it all, or so I thought. I wondered why anyone like me with at least above-average intelligence should take advice from someone with half my age and experience. I could not have been more wrong.

When I finally met with a counselor, I literally clung to every word she uttered like a baby learning to speak. Every time I felt negative thoughts and feelings creep into my prefrontal cortex, I could hear my counselor's reassuring voice in my head, and I was able to relax. The techniques she taught me and the words she spoke, while probably innocuous to her, were life-altering to me. For example, I thought anxiety was something visible that needed to be hidden. The more I worried about blowing my anxious cover, the more anxious I became. She told me it was not, and I suddenly was unafraid to face people, believing I had things under control. Her simple but profound assurances were just the antidotal therapy I needed.

I realize now no one is immune from unexpected change and the resultant anxiety and depression that often accompanies it. One's station or status in life has no correlation to what is really happening in one's mind. I also learned there is no shame or weakness in seeking help from wherever one can get it. Again, it is no overstatement to say the relationships I formed with my neighborhood grocer, dry-cleaner, a few caring friends, and the people who truly loved and cared about me meant the difference between life and death.

Though the counseling helped, in my bathroom still resides a veritable pharmacy replete with pre-scription drugs, supplements, CBD, and a panoply of other *pharmaceuticals* as a memorial to my prior state of mind. My initial plan was to go it alone. I had been on a desperate quest to find the one pill or cocktail of pills that would serve as a talisman for all that ailed me. What I did not realize is nothing in my *pharmacy* was ever designed to solve my crisis. They served only as a crutch I could rely on to set my mind at ease. The cure I sought had to come from within me.

Change is difficult for anyone, whether because of a retirement from a lifelong career, the death of a loved one, or divorce. My change was divorce after thirty-one years of marriage. My identity was that of a husband, a father, and an all-around family man. Although I was far from the perfect husband (as if that exists), I felt like I had been a great provider and father. I worked hard, achieved a lot, sent both of my children to prestigious universities, and paid for everything they ever wanted and even things they never thought about. Even as I write this, I am still paying for my children's cellphone bills and student loans. I do not have the heart to tell them they must assume their own expenses. I guess subconsciously a part of me is clinging to the remnants of my fatherly caregiver role, even if it isn't financially necessary seeing that they both have lucrative jobs.

Our family took at least two major vacations a year and they were not just ordinary vacations. These were trips to Europe, the Caribbean, and across the United States. I say that not to boast but to merely point out that my family meant everything to me. The memories we forged meant far more to me than padding my retirement account.

During my darkest days, I was so incredibly angry with my wife for leaving me, although I cannot say I really blamed her. Throughout our marriage, I used to say I loved my family so much that, like a secret service agent protecting a president, I would stand in the line of fire to take bullets for my wife, my son, and my daughter. Months after my wife left the home and moved in with her mother, and in a fit of rage, I declared I would only take bullets for two. I excluded her.

I suspect that meant little to her, but this statement was emblematic of everything I held dear. I would protect my family even against an assassin's bullet. My wife was in so many ways my rock and protecting her came with my job as husband and caregiver. She gave me the strength to believe in myself, but that rock had been pulverized.

Samson of the Old Testament found his strength through his long hair. As some know, Samson was betrayed by his Philistine lover, Delilah, who cut his hair as he slept. Consequently, he lost his strength. Moving ahead a few thousand years, I felt that when my wife left for good, she figuratively gave me a buzz cut. I had not only lost my strength but also my self-confidence, and my reason to get out of bed every day. Even though I was the one who committed the final act of betrayal, I still blamed my wife for leaving me and putting me in the position where my life was in shambles.

I arrived at the title *Identity Crisis* after much soul searching. A few times in my life I had gone through crises, but nothing like this—a crisis of existential proportions. This crisis felt different because it was different. I truly lost my identity; I lost my reason for working and for living. At age sixty, I had nothing to prove and nothing to gain, and my biggest fear was that I would spend the rest of my life alone. In my mind, I had created a juggernaut that was bigger than I could handle. For the first time in thirty-one years, I was alone without a partner or even so much as a magnetic compass to guide me. I was left to make decisions for myself, which was never my strong suit.

I am happy to say as of this writing, my anxiety and depression have substantially subsided, although I had experienced a few episodes while writing this book and reliving my story. During my process of healing, I attempted to remove parts of my past that failed to serve my goal of surrounding myself with positive thinkers and substantive people. I am still creating a new normal for myself, but I finally see the proverbial light at the end of what was a very dark, bleak, and unforgiving tunnel.

I hope my story will be an inspiration to others going through the same or similar circumstances. I also hope we can finally set aside the notion that mental health issues are a sign of weakness. I believe there is no one stronger than I am at this very moment; I sincerely believe that. I have been tested in unimaginable ways, and while I didn't pass with flying colors, I still passed. That is the most important part—I passed and lived to write about it.

I am still living and breathing by the grace of God, without whom I am nothing. God was present with me throughout this ordeal and He gave me the strength to carry on when I wanted to give up.

I also credit my children, who, unbeknownst to them, were the primary reasons I fought like hell to live. I knew first-hand how suicide affected a family after my brother, Scott, committed suicide at age nineteen. Suicide is not the legacy that I wanted to leave for my children. My children love and adore me as I do them and I wanted to direct my focus away from myself and my problems and toward them.

In many ways, Scott saved my life. Scott was the baby of the family. Chronologically, he was several years younger than my siblings and I. The rest of us had moved out of the house and on with our lives, leaving Scott to fend for himself. I was never particularly close to Scott because he was essentially in a different peer group. We were all stunned to learn that he had taken a pistol, laid in his bathtub, and fired a bullet through his head. His suicide inalterably changed my family.

Looking back, however, Scott had given us all clues. We were just too preoccupied to see them. In my case, Scott called every SCUBA-diving facility in the Raleigh-Durham area until he found the one instructing me on one of my shallow-water qualifying dives. On that particular Saturday, as I reached the surface of the water within the rock-quarry, I was startled to see Scott standing on the rocky shoreline. I wondered how he knew where I would be, but miraculously, he found me. He followed me back to the dive shop and we talked briefly at the shop, but about nothing in-depth or serious. Six days later, Scott was dead. It was only then I realized Scott was reaching out for help. I just didn't recognize it until it was too late.

My family was never close after Scott's death, and large family gatherings came to a grinding halt. Understandably, my parents had a difficult time inviting everyone home, considering Scott's noticeable absence. Many still living recall where they were when President Kennedy was shot or the World Trade Center and Pentagon were attacked. Likewise, each of my family members recalls where they were and what they were doing when they heard Scott shot himself. We never believed suicide could happen in our family, and yet it did.

My love of fitness, even with sometimes half-assed workouts, also deserves credit for saving my life. If not for that, I would have had nowhere to go to clear my head and the loneliness would have driven me crazier. I also had a handful of very close friends (including the aforementioned cashier, dry-cleaner, and a couple of women I met on dating apps), who I could call day or night. Most importantly, I met a woman from Ecuador who showed me what it is to love and be loved again. We took a chance at love during a time when our lives were unsettled and tumultuous. I was alone in my marital home, and she was living with her daughter, having recently separated from her second husband. We spent a lot of time together and I felt better than I had in decades. We laughed together, cried together, and propped up each other.

Strangely enough, throughout my periods of depression, I retreated from most of my family members. As I previously mentioned, I always felt like a burden, regardless of whether I was. I can say without equivocation that apart from the select few people who entered my life at just the right time and a few activities to keep me grounded as much as possible, this book would not have been written because I would not have been alive to write it.

CHAPTER 3

THE GOOD OLD DAYS

I was born the fifth child out of seven to an Air Force Non-Commissioned Officer. My father was a boom operator, which meant he engaged in air-to-air refueling. A jet had a limited fuel supply and to continue its mission and to stay airborne, it needed periodic refueling. My father's job was to maneuver the boom pod to the intake port of fighter jets flying at altitudes of 40,000 feet. I remember watching home movies of my father refueling F-4 Phantom fighter jets over Vietnam. He filmed from the boom pod of his KC-135 Stratotanker. In the movies, I could see craters dotting the landscape below where B-52 Stratofortress bombers had carpet-bombed areas occupied by the Vietcong.

My life was simple and ordinary, but my older siblings played a significant role in guiding me. My older brothers and sisters occasionally put my parents through purgatory, if not outright hell, and I was trying not to follow in their footsteps. To be honest, they were probably far better than most children today. They were just doing what teenagers often do—engage in mischief and an occasional petty crime.

My eagerness to please my parents was both good and bad. I tried to do the things I thought a *good child* would do and, in return, I was not only spared the wrath of my parents but also a trip to see the local magistrate. I cannot say I know the full extent of what my parents went through, but I later heard stories about how they had to sell precious mementos to pay lawyer fees, court costs, fines, etc. It was never my intention to make them sell anything else or to cause them any more angst.

However, had I been a little more rebellious and incurred a little more failure and a little less success, maybe I would have acquired the coping skills to handle much of the larger issues thrown at me. For example, I achieved the rank of Eagle Scout when my two older brothers dropped out. In a certain way, I always felt like I was my parent's last best hope, and I tried to do things that would please them, even though I had no real desire to do certain things. I guess I was just different: the *red-headed stepchild* minus the step. It was often said I must have been adopted because I neither looked nor acted like anyone else in my family.

The ubiquitous feeling of being the *golden child* was my guidepost. But this was a position I neither sought for myself nor desired and yet it caused me to achieve success. It also saddled me with a burden I still carry to this day. That burden—the burden to get things right one hundred percent of the time; the burden to succeed and never fail—added a mountain of stress to me I am only now realizing.

Beginning at age twelve, I started working in the tobacco fields all day every day in the summer. Often the temperatures in the fields reached one-hundred degrees with extremely high humidity. Cropping tobacco was hard, dirty work, and every night in the shower took about an hour to clean off tobacco gum that clung to the hairs on my arms. I believe few children at twelve or of any age would choose to do that sort of manual labor now.

My brothers and I were the last of a dying breed who were picked up at *O-dark-30* in the back of a pickup truck bed and who worked from sunrise to sunset in squelching temperatures and unbearable humidity with only a few breaks for an RC Cola, a pack of peanut butter or cheese nabs, and a Moon Pie. Those were the good old days and yet one could not pay me enough to relive them. I have grown too accustomed to air conditioning and a plush chair. My brothers and I used our money to buy our own school clothes and supplies. At first, this was voluntary, but later it became compulsory, as my parents saw a way to lighten their financial burden.

College was a topic that seldom came up in my house. I think as a matter of affordability, our family never viewed college as a viable option for my siblings or me. My mother had her teaching degree from Florida State University and my maternal grandmother had her undergraduate degree from Adelphi University in New York and her master's degree from East Carolina University.

Despite the lack of discussion and finances, I somehow felt impelled to go to college, even though I was flying by the seat of my pants. I qualified for a few grants and loans to get me through. I recall a brief mention of the necessity to take the Scholastic Aptitude Test (SAT), although I never prepared to take it and did not fully understand its significance in the college admissions process. I knew nothing about the test and was not prepared for it, yet my score was good enough to get me into a four-year college.

I will never forget checking into college on the first day. My mother could not have been prouder. We made our way into the student union and the bookstore, where my sweet mother insisted on buying me a tee shirt or sweatshirt with my college name emblazoned on the front. I refused to take her up on her offer, because I was convinced I would not make it past the first semester. In my mind, college was for people far smarter than I. I felt I was not college material.

I later found out that not only was I college material, but I excelled in college, making the Dean's List several semesters and ultimately winning a scholarship for being the most outstanding musician. If I had bet against my chances of success, which I essentially did, I would have lost. I took out loans in my name that needed to be paid back with some form of employment. This loomed large in my mind and was undoubtedly the impetus for my success.

I could always rely on my English grammar skills. My vocabulary was not particularly impressive, but I understood sentence structure and felt I was a creative writer. I attribute this to my high school English teacher, who instilled in me the importance of speaking and writing well. He is still the only teacher I have ever heard of who made his students memorize and recite in class Geoffrey Chaucer's (1342-1400)[1] General Prologue to the Canterbury Tales in Old English. Forty-five years later, I still recall these opening lines:

Whan that Aprill with his shoures soote
The droghte of March hath perced to the roote,
And bathed every veyne in swich licour
Of which vertu engendred is the flour;

On one occasion in college, I took a grammar exam. I felt I had aced it but, to my surprise, I received a failing grade. I went to my professor to find out how this was possible. He looked at his grading key and discovered it was completely incorrect or his student assistant had used the wrong key. My exam was correct and, after further review, he changed my grade from an F to an A.

After college, I got my first real break when the principal for Dunn Middle School in Dunn, North Carolina, contacted me about a temporary general music position. The full-time teacher had some sort of serious surgery and was convalescing for six months. As luck would have it (at least as far as I was concerned), she chose to stay out for the remainder of the year and then permanently. I was able to keep the position on a full-time basis. I continued to work at Dunn Middle School for one additional year until I was offered an assistant band director position.

I will never forget that in 1984, my starting salary as a general music teacher was a paltry $13,500.00 a year. With that meager pay, I had to pay for housing, food, clothing, and student loans. I also had a broken-down car that needed a lot of mechanical attention. When I bought that car from one of my brothers-in-law who was in the car business, he told me it had been garage kept, which is usually a code meaning a car was well-maintained. After driving that car for only a month, I questioned whether garage kept meant mechanic's garage kept. This car was literally a broken-down piece of crap.

One could get seasick riding in that car. The suspension was so defective that the car drove like a boat encountering three-to-four-foot seas. I probably should have provided barf bags to my passengers. The radio did not work either and whenever it rained, water leaked inside. The car smelled like mildew and mold, and I did not have the money for a professional repair. I bought a tube of silicone to seal the windshield to prevent it from leaking, but that was useless. I eventually used a roll of brown packaging tape all around the seals of the windshield and from that moment on, the car was referred to as the tape mobile.

The challenges I faced financially as a young adult were not unlike the ones I faced growing up. To make ends meet on a beginning teacher's salary, I took up residence at the home of a very sweet elderly woman. I lived on the second floor, and she lived on the first. The biggest treat was being invited to sit with her at her dining room table, usually on a Sunday afternoon for a home-cooked meal typically consisting of pork neck bones and rice. To me, this was literally living high on the hog. Again, I knew no better. In fact, once I got my own place, I continued to shop for pork neck bones. The pork was tasty, tender and, above all, affordable. Only years later did I really think about what I was eating and before I could afford a more choice cut of pork.

As I entered the dating world in earnest, the elderly woman with whom I shared residency voiced dissatisfaction with women I would bring home from time to time. The women never caused any problems. I think it was simply a matter of not knowing who was entering or exiting her home late at night or early in the morning. I decided I needed to move out.

My move also coincided with my new position as assistant band director. I found a somewhat affordable place to live a short distance from my boarding house. My bachelor pad was a single-wide mobile home in Buies Creek, North Carolina. Buies Creek is the home to Campbell University (*nee* Campbell College). I enjoyed living near Campbell because it afforded me the opportunity to use the weight room and I could easily attend sporting events. I was also able to meet new people who were attending the College.

My workout buddy still teases me to this day about the trailer and jokingly refers to it as a Superfund site for reasons that should need no further explanation. I truly was living in the single man's paradise. I had my own place and a never-ending supply of young female suiters from which to choose. Although I had virtually no money, it did not seem to matter to me or to the girls I invited to stay at my humble abode. I had a place to call my own and there were no resident assistants or elderly women to tell me who I could invite.

The ultimate bachelor pad was nothing like one might expect. This was arguably the most dilapidated trailer one can imagine. It literally had several broken panes of glass and others that improperly functioned. Had Buies Creek been a hotbed of criminal activity, I would have been a prime target. With that trailer, there would have been no breaking and entering, only entering. The breaking had already occurred.

One night I called the fire department because I smelled something burning inside. It was only the heater malfunctioning that could have caused the trailer to burn up in under a minute with me inside. No big deal. I asked several times for my *landlord* (and that is being kind) to make the repairs and, though he promised he would, those promises went unfulfilled. I mean, there are landlords, slumlords, and then there was this guy, the lowest of all slumlords—a bumlord. The trailer itself was a deathtrap and honestly needed to be chopped up and placed into a massive trash compactor.

But in real estate, everything is about location, location, location, and I felt I had the perfect location. If location meant sacrificing certain creature comforts such as heat, working windows, entire panes of glass, usable appliances, and risking my life, so be it; I just had to improvise.

I bought a large kerosene heater for the living room and used it as a heat source. As long as my guests and I huddled within a three-foot radius of this noxious fume-emitting beast, we could stay toasty warm. I moved the heater to my bedroom whenever I was ready to sleep and kept that heater operating at full capacity. It is a wonder I survived the winters with the effervescent scent of kerosine and undetectable carbon monoxide wafting throughout the trailer. Perhaps it was a blessing my *bumlord* never fixed the broken windows, thus allowing carcinogenic and asphyxiating strong fumes to escape while allowing just enough fresh air to enter my lungs to keep me alive. As of this writing, my lungs are cancer free. How? I could not tell you.

As decrepit as that trailer was, I took pride in it. It was the first place in some sense I could call my own. I once tried to clean the green mildew off the sides of what was supposed to be its white facade. The trouble was I could not afford a ladder, so only the bottom two-thirds of the trailer were restored to its semi-white condition while the top one-third remained green. I also added gravel to the parking spot so I would not have to walk-in ankle-deep water to get into my car following a heavy rain storm. It did not work and standing rainwater soaked my feet up to my ankles. All these projects were DIY because I did not have the financial re-sources to hire a professional to level the parking spot, repair the windows, etc. Asking my *bumlord* to do anything was pointless.

By most economic metrics, I was poor. Maybe I was not Martinique, Belize, or Zimbabwe poor, but by the United States' standards, I was poor. I often found myself scrounging around the floorboards of my car, hoping I could cobble together enough loose change that had fallen to buy three hotdogs for a dollar, the going rate at a local fast-food joint. That was my reality, but it engrained in me the feelings of wanting to get out as soon as I could and never wanting to return.

To this very day and to an unhealthy degree, I think about money. I firmly believe the fear of returning to poverty is the fuel that drives my ambition. I had no choice but to be successful. If my life had been summed up on a bumper sticker, it might say *success at any cost.* I determined long ago I was not going back to that broken down trailer or driving another tape mobile. And, as tasty as they were, I sure as hell was not planning to shop for more pork neck bones.

Whenever I was *triggered (discussed more thoroughly in Chapter 7),* a term used in psychology referring to the deleterious effects certain memories can have on the mind again, I panicked. The reality hit me that I had used up my surplus of disposable cash. For the first time since the start of my law practice, I felt the gears slipping on my financial rack and pinion. My knee jerk reaction was first to cut back my secretary's hours and cancel my home cable television service.

I always felt a little stressed relying on the public to earn a living, but in the early days, we had a backup plan. That plan went by two names: buzzard's row and vulture's row—names given to the lineup of attorneys who sat hoping the duty judge would hand them a piece of fresh criminal litigation roadkill. To simplify this discussion, I will refer to the rows only as either vulture's row or the Row.

Prior to the initiation of the Public Defender (PD) system, courts relied exclusively on private attorneys to essentially perform *pro bono* services to indigent defendants. As any civic-minded person knows, the Constitution provides all people with the right to legal counsel through the 6th Amendment. In the past, Virginia courts constructed a method for assigning attorneys to those who could not afford to hire their own and thus, vulture's row was spawned.

In its heyday, the Row was nothing more than chairs lining the walls around the well of the courtroom. Attorneys would rush to do whatever cases they had to do before Attorney Determination and Trial Dates (ADATs) began. During ADATs, the court paraded defendants before the court one-by-one and formally advised them of their charges. If those charges carried the possibility of a jail or prison sentence, the court informed them of their right to counsel under the 6th Amendment and presented three options: they could waive their right to counsel, hire their own counsel, or request appointed counsel if they met the financial parameters for indigence (i.e. stone cold broke). If counsel was appointed for the defendant or they waived their right to counsel, the trial date would be set right then and there. Otherwise, the case was set on a control date to give the defendant time to hire his own attorney, after which the trial date was set.

Usually, the duty judge handling ADATs started with the chair closest to him. If a defendant requested court-appointed counsel and met the criteria, the judge assigned cases in succession, e.g., seat 1, seat 2, seat 3, and so on until all cases were distributed. The system was essentially first-come, first-served. If ten attorneys sat on vulture's row and only seven cases were available on a particular day, three attorneys would have no raw meat that day and would simply return the following day, hoping to get a choicer spot on *the Row*.

On a couple of occasions, fights nearly broke out among attorneys because those who staked their spot by piling notepads and case files on a seat of the chair often returned to find their chair had been commandeered by another attorney. If the attorney had not returned to *the Row* near the start of the assignment process, items were removed, and the spot was assumed by another attorney. That did not sit well with the attorney who then found himself forced to sit at the end of *the Row* and left to potentially miss out on the few scraps of criminal law innards meted out that day. The person who moved someone's belongings could have literally cost the other attorney thousands of dollars.

The fee paid by the Commonwealth of Virginia for most court-appointed cases was ninety dollars an hour up to a statutory maximum, usually four hundred and forty-five dollars per felony. If one was lucky and got appointed to a defendant who had three felonies, his fee would be capped at four hundred and forty-five dollars multiplied by three for a total of $1,335.00.

This was no slim pickings as any attorney who got assigned to a six-felony case could potentially make $2,670.00 and the beauty was no limitations were set on how many days a person could sit on *the Row* or how many cases one could be assigned. Although the fee was less than one could receive from an actual paying client, court-appointed fees were often aggregated into a sizable check that seemed to arrive at the most opportune times.

Court-appointed cases were the closest thing to a paycheck a sole practitioner could get. It was never a lot of money, but funds were guaranteed to be paid and indigent defendants were never in short supply. Once the PD's office came in, the court-appointed work was largely vaporized overnight leaving only conflict-of-interest cases and cases with multiple codefendants. This meant that court appointed attorneys lost a reliable and predictable annual income of about $50,000 without much notice.

The pressure to maintain a business became even more stressful as we were now missing our *paychecks*. I know many who attempted private practice and quickly fizzled out. They could not stand the stress of going without a steady revenue source. They gave it a try but quickly went back to the safety and security of bi-weekly paychecks.

At the precise time I was being triggered, I realized that my business had stalled. The phones were not ringing, and I was pulling in no business. With *the Row* largely disbanded and little to no retained business, I essentially had no viable law practice, but my bills were ubiquitous. My business was my fourth house that, at that moment, converted from an asset to a liability. My office needed electricity, computers, a secretary, insurance, and supplies. Rent also had to be paid. I suddenly realized I had a lot more capital outgoing than incoming.

Something had to give, and it was my mind that gave. I previously discussed the other pressures I was under, and this was yet another massive pressure stacked on top. Looking back, I would say my life and career were like a giant game of Jenga where certain blocks—bills to be exact—were pulled out and placed on top of one another until the whole thing teetered and crashed.

CHAPTER 4
THE WAY WE WERE

My ex-wife and I met in Washington, DC. In July 1989. I had only recently been commissioned as an Ensign from Coast Guard Officer Candidate School in Yorktown, Virginia, after five months of intense training. My first duty assignment was the National Response Center (NRC) in Washington, DC. The NRC was tasked with taking reports of oil discharges and chemical releases within the navigable waterways of the entire United States and its territories. We were essentially the command center for the National Response Team that included the Cabinet Secretaries of all federal agencies and the Whitehouse Situation Room.

Prior to my assignment at the NRC, my ex-wife moved to Washington, DC to take a second-grade teaching position at an elementary school in one of the worst parts of DC. Everyday teachers had to canvas the playground in search of syringes and used condoms. The sound of gunshots was commonplace.

My ex-wife took the position largely for a change of pace but also to get a break from her controlling father. She desired autonomy and independence, and being four hours away provided that. Every day she returned home, I breathed a sigh of relief. Let us just say, in southeast Washington, she stood out among her colleagues and students. One of her students was seen wandering around the school one day looking for his classroom and when he was asked who his teacher was, he said Mrs. White. The other teacher knew exactly who his teacher was and where to take him.

Both of us had apartments in the same complex in Southwest Washington. The complex itself was a roach-infested crap hole, and that is being kind. It was common to see dozens of cockroaches scamper into seclusion whenever the lights of the apartment were turned on. But our meeting was destiny.

I had only been in the complex for a month or so when I saw this beautiful, petite, young woman—a spitting image of the young Demi Moore—in the elevator with her aunt and young cousin. She caught my eye, and I glanced over her way in what I thought was a discreet manner, though apparently not discreet enough. As we were riding to the ground floor, her aunt noticed me staring and said, *You can say hello, you know.* In about as country a twang as one can imagine, I responded, *Well, she sure looks mighty good.* I was so countrified that I would have made Buck Owens and Dwight Yoakam sound like Yankees.

Once we hit the ground floor, she stepped out with her aunt and cousin, and then I exited. That was the extent of the chivalry and the conversation, and I kicked myself for not engaging her further or getting her personal information. Moments after I met her, I called just about everyone I knew and said, I just met Demi Moore's twin sister. I feel certain she too called her friends about some guy with charisma, good looks, a great physique, and who was witty and charming. But enough about Bruce Willis.

After a little thought, I concluded there was a sure-fire pathway to meeting her again. I had befriended the security guard in the lobby, and I knew he saw everyone coming and going. I talked him into telling her the guy she saw in the elevator was interested in her. I gave him her description, and he said whenever he saw her, he would tell her I wanted to meet again.

Whenever I next saw the security guard, he told me he had passed along my message. As luck would have it, one day I saw her pull into the parking lot in her silver Toyota Tercel and I quickly took the elevator to the ground floor to *coincidentally* run into her. I assisted her in carrying her groceries to her apartment. We talked a while, and we were an item from that moment on.

I am just a simple country boy from North Carolina, and that is what she loved about me. She is a New Yorker but the antithesis of the stereotypical smooth talking city slicker from New York City. You would never guess that she came from financial means. She was not a big spender, and she was humble almost to a fault, at least when it came to her family and friends.

Once we started dating in earnest, we talked and laughed about our first encounter in the elevator, especially my deep country twang and my cutoff shorts with frayed threads hanging two inches below the bottom. Her cousin saw those shorts and teased me incessantly by calling them *Daisy Dukes*. Anyone old enough to remember the Dukes of Hazard on television knows exactly what he meant. I was a hot mess, but she did not seem to care.

We also spoke about the security guard and his role in matchmaking. We affectionately referred to him as our black angel. Our meeting felt like a match made in heaven. Later, as our relationship began to unravel like the bottom of my cutoff shorts, we jokingly referred to him as our black devil.

Within one year from our meeting, we were married. In those days, little consideration was given to anything except that we were young and attracted to each other. Our marriage had its ups and downs like any marriage, I suppose. I could have done many things differently and better. I have promised myself that for any future relationship, I will do my best to live up to that ideal.

I think we both tried to make our marriage work in different ways. Neither of us wanted it to end, but the love had just died for a variety of reasons, most of which will remain personal to us. I harbored a lot of resentment toward her for reasons that also will not be discussed out of respect for ourselves and our children. I should have let the animosity I felt die naturally, but I always thought my marriage would be everlasting, so I failed to work on myself and our relationship until it was too late.

In her zeal to satisfy everyone, which is her nature, my ex-wife would alter our plans so as not to offend anyone, even if those plans were essentially set in stone. Near the end of our marriage, I used to jokingly say, Elon Musk could invite us to blast off on a SpaceX rocket, which of course would be a once in a lifetime opportunity. But if her family later invited us to a birthday party for one of her nephews, she would forgo the rocket trip in favor of the party. I did not always agree with her decisions that seemed malleable and I clearly would have opted for a rocket trip. But that was my ex-wife. She put family first come hell, high water, or a rocket trip on a SpaceX Falcon 9.

As we neared the end of our nuptial, we each began doing more and more things on our own. I should have seen that as the inevitable death knell of our lengthy marriage, but I just could not imagine our marriage would end. Neither one of us was truly happy, but I think we each figured happiness was overrated. Besides, we had two children together and several joint real estate investments that would seemingly require Moses to part.

The two most incredible results of our thirty-one-year marriage are our two beautiful and intelligent children. We could not be more blessed. They never gave us a minute of trouble at any stage of their lives and showered us with infinite joy. They are so incredibly gifted and talented in every respect, from academic to extracurricular. I take tremendous pride in knowing we are responsible for creating two great people who will contribute significantly to society and who have already accomplished so much in such a short period of time. I am immensely proud not only to call them my children but also my best friends and, because of this ordeal, saviors.

If my ex-wife and I made any serious missteps during the child rearing days, it was placing our children ahead of ourselves. As I just mentioned, we have amazing children, but we should have ensured we took our own vacations or at least had date nights without the children. We put everything into our children, from financial resources to our free time. We love the way our children matured, but if I had a do-over, I would strike more of a balance between doing for the children and doting over my wife. I failed miserably in that regard.

Chivalry may not have been dead, but it was on life support in my marriage. If I had the chance for a reprise, I would open and close the car door regardless of the convenience of having a key FOB, pull out her chair at a restaurant, and put away my cellular device. I would listen and pay attention as she talked about her day, ask questions about her life, and try not to find fault or upbraid her at every opportunity over trivial things.

I wore my wedding ring with pride for nearly 31 years. I never removed it. In fact, my fingers had gotten fatter over the years and the ring caused a semi-permanent indention in my ring finger. I am not sure I could have removed it even if I chose to. But if you believe in foreshadowing, my ring was symbolic.

Months before our separation, I had periods of edema that went from my feet to my arms and ultimately to my hands. To this day, I have no logical explanation for it. The edema left my body as quickly as it entered and has never returned since, but for that period I ended up in the emergency room because my circulation was being restricted.

My fingers were so swollen the doctor needed to cut off my wedding ring or I might have lost my finger. I had no sensible option but to agree. After 31 years, my ring not only came off but was cut off, and remained off my ring finger from that day forward.

Similarly, my ex-wife had a nearly flawless 1.3 carat diamond engagement ring I bought her in 1990. Near the end of our marriage, that diamond broke free from its prongs and was lost for a short time. Only repeated prayers to St. Anthony of Padua brought it back. The venerable St. Anthony, the Patron Saint for lost articles, is credited with performing miracles involving lost people and lost things. With the help of St. Anthony, my ex-wife found the diamond, but we never had it re-mounted. I believe these two incidents portended what would follow a short time later.

CHAPTER 5
THE ROOT OF ALL EVIL

I grew up in what I consider a normal family, whatever that means. We had the basics—a roof over our heads and food on the table. To me, that was enough. I did not know any better. If I lived in a temperature-controlled environment, however cramped, and could satisfy my appetite, I felt I needed little else.

We always had a bountiful Christmas. Having six siblings and two parents always meant plenty of presents stacked under our Christmas tree. My parents made little money and to provide any sort of festive Yuletide celebration took great financial sacrifice and yet sacrifice they did.

Perhaps one of the most memorable gifts was the bicycle that was recycled every year. This bicycle started out new when my oldest sister received it, but as the years went by and she outgrew it, the bicycle was handed down to the next in line. Of course, before it made its way to the next person, it always got a complete overhaul with a new paint job and whatever accouterments were needed to make it gleam again.

My father always did an amazing job of making that bicycle look new, but as good a mechanic as my father was, wear and tear eventually took its toll. I am not sure at what point that bicycle took on a nickname and who named it. I only recall after several years of use, *Shabby* became its endearing sobriquet. The biggest joke at Christmas was waiting for Shabby to make its grand appearance to its rightful new "owner." I put the word owner in quotation marks only because, in *legal parlance*, the relationship between us and that bicycle was more of a bailment than true ownership.

We had a limited period to use of the bicycle (one year to be exact) and we knew we had better maximize our time with Shabby before it was handed down to the next person. I was the fifth bailee to ride Shabby. The funny thing is, you would have thought I had gotten a BMW for Christmas. I had Shabby for a whole year, much to the envy of everyone, even those who preceded me. *Shabby* was like the present-day Flat Stanley.

Flat Stanley did not start out flat but being flat had its advantages. He could go anywhere and visit anyone any time he was brought along. In a word, he had freedom. Likewise, Shabby wasn't always Shabby, and it too represented freedom. Shabby afforded us the opportunity to go anywhere at any time. No one was upset if Shabby was dinged, dented, scratched, or left in the rain to rust because we all knew after our bailment expired, our dad would magically restore the iridescence of old Shabby.

Shabby is just one example of how to make the most out of a little. I feel certain feeding and clothing nine people on a non-commissioned officer's salary gave my parents insomnia and anxiety. I do not know how they achieved that feat, but as I got older, I appreciated it more and more.

Grocery shopping required at least two carts filled well over the brim. Groceries were often cantilevered over the shopping carts. A dozen or so loaves of bread, and at least six dozen eggs were common. But we never had food items beyond the basics and sometimes we did not have those. Any-time the station wagon was backed up, it was an all-hands-on-deck moment to take the bags from the car to the kitchen. It was also an exciting time as we got to see just what provisions we could expect in the coming week.

I grew up on powdered milk and lasagna filled with cottage cheese, not ricotta, both of which I now find grotesque. But at that point in my life, I knew no difference. We were well fed and usually didn't go hungry, but there were times late at night when we would root around the kitchen looking for something to nibble on and that's usually when we heard *the kitchen is closed* bellowing from the master bedroom.

One thing that shaped my way of thinking about money was knowing the cost of groceries. There was never a time when we were not told how much money had been shelled out for groceries right down to the cents. Subconsciously, it made me extremely cognizant of the costs of everything. Later in life, I tried to avoid thinking about costs, yet I found myself being exactly like my parents. Nearly every decision and every purchase I ever made was only after an extensive cost analysis that I loudly proclaimed.

Growing up with limited resources was not without its funny moments. A story that is part of our family lore involves pork chops. For reasons we still do not understand, my mother always made ten pork chops for the nine of us. She placed all ten on a platter in the center of the table. All eyes were fixated on that tenth pork chop. Without any regard for anyone else, we ravaged our given pork chop so we could rightfully (or so we thought) be the first to lay claim to the tenth. This was usually accomplished by taking one's fork and stabbing the pork chop in its juicy epicenter.

Much like an explorer shoves a flag into the ground to stake his claim to territory, that fork was an affirmation of ownership. The only thing left to do at that point was to ask the obligatory and somewhat rhetorical question: Does anyone want this? Of course, the answer was no for two distinct reasons: First, it would have been rude to say yes and second, no one wanted the pork chop after someone else's used fork had penetrated the pork chop's Shake 'n Bake crusty facade. My dad was the final arbiter of all things culinary. Many times, I heard him angrily ask the one laying claim why he or she felt entitled to that pork chop. That was usually followed by a methodical withdrawal of the fork, silence, and a tinge of disappointment that lasted until the next meal.

As fondly as I remember these things now, they planted seeds in me that everything had not just a monetary price, but a price calculated in toil and sweat. We were mostly poor, and we were constantly reminded of how hard my father worked to provide. We qualified for free lunches in school, but because my dad was too prideful to accept anything free, he opted for the reduced lunch. Many days, we brought lunch from home in generic rubber made containers versus the popular Superman or Spiderman lunchboxes of those times. We were teased quite a lot in school about those containers. I somehow came into possession of a true lunchbox, complete with a metal thermos. One of the few fights I ever had in school centered around that lunchbox.

Although my memory of this incident is somewhat sketchy, I recall a boy snatching my lunchbox and then damaging it. That sent me into a fit of rage. I do not recall much about the fight, but I do recall eventually retrieving my lunchbox. Whatever contusions I received were nothing more than battle scars. I was entrusted with not just any lunchbox, but a superhero lunchbox, and I had an obligation to uphold the integrity of what that stood for. Mine was not just any fight, but a fight for truth, justice, and the American way. If Superman would not have cowered in that instant, neither would I.

As I grew older, I realized just how underprivileged we really were. As I began earning my own money, I knew being impoverished was not for me. I was not going back there come hell or high water. Although the Bible says in 1 Timothy 6:10 that the love of money is the root of all evil (not money itself), to me, money represented freedom— freedom to travel, freedom to provide my children with all the trappings my success could allow, and the ability to retire. Money gave me the ability to do or have the things I wanted whenever I wanted them and to be benevolent toward my children— something my parents were unable to do with my siblings or me, with a few exceptions. I can't say I love money, but if given the choice of having money or not, I would most certainly prefer the former.

But on a warm summer day at a friend's wedding with my wife and daughter no less, money took center stage and I experienced what I now know are *triggers*. In a few short hours, and without realizing it, my mind veered off course to a perilous place. I was in full-blown panic mode. My fight-or-flight instincts were in hyperdrive. Reality hit me at that wedding that my wife was threatening to take all I had built, thus rendering me insolvent and bringing me back to the time I had to fight for my lunchbox.

In an instant, I became that ten-year-old little boy who had nothing and who later swore he would never go back to the impoverished place from whence he came. It was one thing to be ten and not know any better, but I was sixty and had achieved more than I could have ever imagined. I saw my ex-wife as an enemy combatant destined to steal the identity I made for myself. I felt I needed to protect that at any cost.

Shortly after the wedding, my ex-wife and I got into some of the most heated arguments I ever had with anyone. I had never spoken to her the way I did on the days that followed the wedding, but it was fight or flight and everything inside me was set to fight mode. In the beginning, I pleaded with her to come home to complete the family, but once I realized my pleas were pointless, my self-preservation instincts kicked into overdrive and propelled me to a higher level of anger.

I had now given up on any sort of reconciliation and had to view her not as my wife, but as a third party out to ruin my life. The conversations we had were ruthless. I saw and heard a side of myself I never knew before. I felt almost possessed as I ruthlessly snapped back at her every justification for ruining my life and its just rewards.

I had an answer for everything. If it is true that *to the victor goes the spoils*, I was prepared to enter the octagon of life to ensure I did not lose. Failure and defeat were not options. Many of the problems in my life centered on money, and I was willing to fight for the life to which I had grown accustomed.

My maternal grandmother once sent all of us to a hifalutin private school. She knew that to rise above and to create a successful future, we needed a *good education*. A good education could be parlayed into more money. Everyone in the school knew we did not belong there. We did not come from money. We were like the Clampetts from the television show The Beverly Hillbillies going to a private school.

The other students bullied us because we were not the children of wealthy socialites. Instead of being dropped off in a Buick Electra 225 or a Mercedes Benz, the luxury cars of that era, we were taken to school in an old worn out Buick Sport Wagon with seating for nine.

Although my grandmother had the best of intentions, she unwittingly placed us all into an environment where we literally had to fight for our survival. Every one of us got into more fights that year than I care to count with the well-to-do rich kids who thumbed their noses at us. But we were like scrappy kids from the Bronx who knew how to survive and defend their honor. If absolute worst came to worst and we were outgunned, so to speak, the rest of us could always rely on our brother Mike to come to our aid.

Mike was physically built to fight. He was short, stocky, muscular, and had a jaw chiseled like the shape and strength of the finest anvil. He was truculent and feared no one. Comparing him to more recent fighters, I would say he was built like Mike Tyson, with fists the size of baseball gloves and the determination of a gladiator. Had he been put into the Roman Coliseum with the lions, it would have been the lions who flinched first.

This may all sound a little hyperbolic, but that is how I viewed him. I saw him in action and heard stories of his putting foes in the hospital. I did not doubt any of these stories for a second. Mike was never one to start a fight, but if provoked enough, he did not hesitate to end one.

My point is money has always been an issue in my life, whether it was due to lack or fear of my hard earned abundance being taken away. Everyone needs money to survive, and I worked extremely hard to acquire it. I had resigned myself to not going back to the days of *Shabby*, the dilapidated trailer, or pork neck bones. I was determined to hold on to as much wealth as possible, not because I wanted to see my ex-wife suffer, but to avoid reverting to the time when I had no money and lived paycheck to paycheck.

Two things are universally true: The love of money is the root of all evil, and money cannot buy happiness. But money is a necessary evil. Here in the United States, we are particularly bad about our work and life balance. We tend to work our whole lives, never grasping what is important. I missed out on golden opportunities to enrich my own life with my immediate and extended family and to teach my children the value of family. I realize now that where the rubber meets the road, it is family who will usually be there for you, not friends. Make no mistake, family may not always be there for you either, as I can attest, but our best opportunities for fulfillment reside with family.

Had my brother, Mark, my own flesh and blood—a man born of the same womb—not moved in with me, I am not at all sure where I would be now. The decisions surrounding his move were mutually beneficial. He got a new place to live, and some financial relief, and I got a brother who loved me unconditionally and who provided the calm voice of reason when my mind veered toward some calamitous destination.

CHAPTER 6
PRESTO CHANGEO

When I really gave my situation a lot of thought and asked myself what it was about my divorce/new life that was so distressing, one day the answer hit me: change. I realize change is difficult for many people to accept. We get comfortable in our situations and find ourselves content whether we really like our present status or not. I was not happy in my marriage, but I was content. However, I would have stuck it out had I been given the choice.

Whether change occurs on the job, because of new technology, new procedures, or unexpected life circumstances, change requires us all to adapt. Adaptation comes easy for some and harder for others. Looking at all the stages of my life, the thing I struggled with the most was change. I think I struggle because I tend to second guess everything I do. What my ex-wife brought to my life above all else was the stability and confidence to handle whatever changes came my way. If she was onboard with the change, I knew I could handle it and that it was a good decision.

The title to this chapter—Presto Changeo—suggests a suddenly occurring change, as if by magic. I forever second-guess myself about every decision I make. I never had any guidance growing up, so nearly all my decisions were made with no one giving advice or playing the role of the devil's advocate. My parents were not the kind of people I could turn to for advice.

I studied for four years to get my teaching degree in music education. However, due to the lack of career advancement and my passion for music being temporarily spoiled, I did not pursue teaching as a long-term career option.

During my teaching years, I befriended a science teacher who was about to retire. I helped him move his things from the school to his home. His residence was a single wide mobile home and his primary material possessions, at least as far as I could see, were a console television set and a stereo receiver with speakers. Whenever I thought about continuing as a teacher, I only had to revisit those visual images in my head and I knew teaching was not for me. I don't consider myself to be particularly materialistic, but I couldn't see working a lifetime and having virtually nothing to show for it.

Another issue that profoundly impacted my decision to leave teaching was my absolute love of music that was not shared by most of my students. I spent many Saturdays poring over musical compositions at the sheet music store and testing out many of the parts on the piano to choose the ones I thought were brimming with musicality. Most of my selections were classic melodies any budding and serious musician needed to have in his repertoire.

I painstakingly filled each folder for each instrument with my new selections and eagerly awaited the arrival of my students. I quickly discovered I was the only one who was imbued with my musical choices. My band only struggled through four or five measures of their sheet music before I was forced to conduct the cutoff and then wait for the obligatory "this sucks." My band was content playing pop music, but anything resembling classical music or standard musical literature was a nonstarter.

The passion I once felt to teach music flowed from my body. I no longer found joy in it. After five years of teaching, I thought I would attempt a career in the military. After all, a Bachelor of Science in music education does not exactly prepare one to tackle the most vexing problems of the day. The military seemed like an obvious choice.

I applied for a position as an officer in the U.S. Navy. My oldest brother, Mike, was in the navy and it seemed like the perfect choice. I cannot recall exactly why I was not a good fit for the navy, although I believe the navy was not accepting direct commission officers at that point in time, but I chalked that up to experience and tried for the Coast Guard.

One was allowed three rejections per application, and I had used up two when the one-page letter arrived, beginning with *congratulations*. I was ecstatic. That was my ticket out of high school music and onward to better and more exciting things. I put in my letter of resignation and began Officer Candidate School (OCS) in Yorktown, Virginia, in 1997.

When I left my teaching position and entered the Coast Guard, I struggled massively with the change. I questioned whether I had made the correct choice in leaving the profession for which I had a college degree and venturing into the uncharted waters of the Coast Guard.

I immediately second-guessed my decision to leave the teaching profession for something I knew virtually nothing about. This wholesale change made me doubt myself because I had no one to discuss it with. Soon after I began my training, I thought if only I could go back to teaching, I would in a heartbeat.

I hated the second half of OCS. I felt I was getting into something way above my skill level and the worry caused me great anxiety. I remember sneaking off to use a private telephone, only to cry to family about how I had ruined my life. Anxiety comes with change and a fear of the unknown. I had no one to assure me that I had the right stuff to be successful.

As it turned out, the change was far better than I could have ever imagined and I went on to excel in significant ways, even getting selected for the highly competitive funded law program. Out of 54 extremely smart and accomplished applicants, I was the one chosen. The funded law program meant the Coast Guard would pay my salary at my then current rank of Lieutenant and would also pay my law school tuition. In essence, I would get paid to attend post-graduate school.

I spent roughly twelve years in the Coast Guard and achieved the rank of Lieutenant Commander before I encountered more change. This time change was even more difficult. I had been given all the choice billets in the Coast Guard and was being groomed for positions of greater rank and responsibilities.

For a variety of reasons, ranging from family issues to billet choices, I resigned my commission and took a job working at a top-tier law firm in Manhattan, New York. I know many people who have struggled to transition from military to civilian life. In the military, one automatically garners certain respect simply by virtue of rank. Subordinates are required to greet officers and customarily salute, and I was required to do the same to more senior officers.

One can easily size someone up by looking at his or her chest of ribbons and metals adorning his uniform. A quick glance at these accouterments says whether the person is a highflyer, average, or below average performer. I was always proud to display the Commendation Medals I was awarded that said I was a top-notch performer, but once I got out of the military, none of those things mattered to me or to anyone. All the customs and courtesies were gone. No one could size me up by looking at my business attire. I was just another *suit*.

The military offers a Transition Assistance Program (TAP) class to provide people exiting the military with the tools necessary to succeed in the civilian sector. TAP helps to a point, but nothing can really prepare one to go from being a big fish in a small pond to a little fish surrounded by a sea of sharks. My identity was gone again, and a momentary crisis ensued. If the truth be told, I have never even framed any of my citations and my once-cherished rack of ribbons and medals is stowed in a small box underneath my bathroom sink.

From almost the moment I began working at the law firm in Manhattan, I knew I had made a mistake. I felt ill-prepared to handle the type of law expected of me. On the second day of my new job, I knocked on my supervisor's door for guidance about a task he assigned me. He appeared to be intensely staring at a document on his desk. Getting no response, I knocked again and to my shock and horror, he looked up from his desk, gave me an angry stare with a clenched jaw, and literally chewed my ass for disturbing him.

It was like the scene from Willy Wonka and the Chocolate Factory where Grandpa Joe was about to leave the chocolate factory and venomously stated his displeasure with Willy Wonka by calling him a cheat and a swindler for dashing poor Charlie's hopes and dreams. Willy Wonka looked away from his desk and brutally tore Grandpa Joe a new one for violating rules and unlawfully taking intellectual property.

Arguably, Uncle Joe deserved that tongue-lashing. After all, he laid in his bed for twenty years, seemingly unable to walk, only suddenly finding his strength and mobility after being enticed by a lifetime supply of chocolate. Meanwhile, young Charlie was delivering newspapers to literally earn the bread to feed his good-for-nothing family. But I hadn't sipped a fizzy lifting drink or secreted an Everlasting Gobstopper. On day two of my new job, I only needed clarification and some tutelage for a multi-million-dollar project entrusted to the firm and assigned to me.

I knew right then and there the transition from military lawyer to civilian lawyer was destined to fail. My boss was as bad as all the type-A personalities I encountered in the Coast Guard all rolled into one. I stuck it out for almost two full years. Then September 11, 2001, brought real estate development to a predictable halt and lawyers in my firm were being laid off in droves. I saw the writing on the wall and hastily made the decision to beat the firm to the punch by seeking employment elsewhere. That decision would prove to be my undoing.

When I first moved to New York, I invested in a gorgeous home in Orange County, New York— Tuxedo to be exact—but my commute was horrific. Even prior to September 11th, the commute was about one and a half hours each way. As if that was not bad enough, after September 11th, the commute was often three hours each way, as each suspicious package had to be inspected and each bus entering Manhattan was surveyed for explosives.

The revelation that I wanted to leave New York together with my family floated like a lead balloon. The person taking the news the hardest was my late father-in-law. I never intended to show him any disrespect by taking his only daughter back to Virginia again, but I needed a change and between the slowdown in the firm's business, my horrendous commute, and my children's overall unhappiness, a return to Hampton Roads, Virginia seemed like the likely destination.

I will never forget the day I drove over to my father-in-law's house to speak with him and hopefully clear the air about the decision to move back to Virginia. He ignored me the entire time. I was in a sense invisible to him. After a reasonable amount of time had passed in silence, I solemnly drove home thinking about how I was responsible for the destruction of his family, not my family, but his.

Shortly after I arrived, he showed up at my house and I answered the knock on the door. He said, *If you really want to talk, let's talk.* I did not do too much talking, but I sat there as he unleashed his venom, telling me he loved everyone in my family but me. He told me I was dead to him. Those words sliced through me as if he were Zorro wielding his sword.

My family had thrived in Virginia two years prior to my exit from the Coast Guard, and we had an incredible group of friends. But after getting pushback, hate, and discontent from my late father-in-law, I reconsidered my decision and sought a job in Morristown, New Jersey.

My ex-wife could see I was not happy, and neither were my children at their tiny, one-class-per-grade school, so we decided to relocate. We sold our beautiful home, and I took an associate position at a law firm in Virginia Beach. That job was doomed from the start. I felt I had no one left in my corner and the anxiety of seemingly ripping apart my ex-wife's family was unbearable.

Maybe deep down I am just a gentle soul who does not like to upset anyone, but the pressures I felt were immense and I believed I had made the worst decision of my life. Just as I was getting back on my feet, one of the partners and my direct supervisor entered my office and informed me I was being laid off. I think they knew something was very off with me from the start and as much as I tried to hide it, my fate was sealed.

One month before my termination, I sought help from a psychiatrist in Virginia Beach to restore my confidence and to reduce my anxiety. Unfortunately, his idea of help was to prescribe and over-prescribe psychotropic medications to where I felt like the offspring of a white walker and the walking dead. I was truly zombified, but I kept slithering forward, dragging all my mental baggage with me.

The psychiatrist then made a near fatal diagnosis. He said I was psychotic. I did not know how psychosis felt, but I did not believe I was psychotic. I considered whatever I was going through to be situational, not chronic, but he said I was psychotic and I thought maybe he was right.

He prescribed an antipsychotic medication, Seroquel, I took only once. I drove home during my lunch break from my office and took one pill. On my way back to the office, I developed the most piercing, excruciating pain in my head I cannot describe. I thought I was having a stroke.

My vision drew faint to the point I could barely see. I was driving thinking I was either going to die from the stroke itself or I was going to crash into another vehicle on the interstate. But either way, I thought my life was going to end behind the wheel of my car.

I must either be the luckiest man to inhabit the planet or God was looking out for me then, because I pulled off the interstate and almost immediately found myself at the emergency entrance to Sentara Leigh Hospital. A short time later, I called my secretary using only touch, as I could not read the digits on my cellular phone. I was rendered temporarily blind. I explained the situation to her and thankfully she picked me up and drove me home.

Following that episode, I took a week of medical leave and spent time at my parents' home, where my mother made valiant efforts to nurse me back to health. During that week, my boss at the law firm called to check on me and my mother frankly said too much. I could hear her speaking with him over the telephone as I laid in bed. She meant no harm and was just being a loving and protective mother, but my boss had to wonder who on earth the firm hired.

Based only on my mother's part of the conversation, she was describing my malady as more mental than physical. I only lasted six months at the new firm as it was obvious to everyone my confidence had not only been deflated but had exploded and crashed like the mighty Hindenburg. And just to clear up any confusion, I am not psychotic, not that there's anything wrong with that.

I will always wonder how well I would have done at the new firm in Virginia Beach had I not first encountered massive backlash and outright vitriol from my father-in-law. I will never know how well I would have done if my father-in-law had simply said something like, "We love you no matter what you do or where you go. We only want you and your family to be happy. You have our unwavering support."

Again, change has never been easy for me, only this time I had to contend with change and discontent on an epic scale. Several years went by before my father-in-law and I got back on speaking terms, and I am not at all sure he ever really cared for me, but for the sake of my children and his daughter it appeared he was able to sheath his invidious sword.

After I lost my job at the new firm in Virginia Beach, I filled out every application I could find, hoping for gainful employment in or out of law. As laughable as it is now, I dropped off my resumé at McDonalds. I just did not care what I did at that moment. I only needed somewhere to go and something to do.

We had a hammock I would lie in while my then wife went to work at a preschool. The hammock should have been a source of relaxation, but was a source of consternation. I quickly jumped out of that hammock and assumed a more proper position the moment I heard my wife pull up. The hardest thing for me was not having a purpose or an identity. I believe the identity of most men is directly linked to their employment. People often ask about your profession after asking your name. Truthfully, I felt emasculated. I thought of myself as a failure and a worthless bum.

After I struck out finding a new job commensurate with my law degree and experience, nothing was left for me to do except open my own practice. I had absolutely no experience running a business, but my time in New York taught me a little about private practice. Opening my own law practice was the furthest thing from my mind, but I had run out of options.

The experience I had on my second day in the Manhattan firm left me feeling like I could not work for anyone else. I often tell people the greatest thing about being my own boss is that the only jerk to whom I must answer is myself. I was also under the misguided assumption that I could come and go as I pleased. I was so wrong. I have never worked longer or harder than as my own boss.

I am not sure how I found out that I could become a part of the system to help indigent defendants.

As I mentioned earlier, this so-called system was affectionally called vulture's or buzzard's row (*the Row*). I will forever be grateful to the few attorneys, particularly the late Randolph Stowe, who took me under their wings and showed me the ropes when they could have resented this guy with a slight New York accent poised to steal a few leftover scraps from vultures who had been on *the Row* far longer.

All the work court-appointed to me became the foundation for my practice. I did not know Virginia law and had never practiced criminal law any-where but in the military. But I diligently worked on those cases far more than I really needed, fig-uring if I did a good enough job and was attentive enough to the court-appointed clients, they would call me back when or if they ever needed an at-torney again. I also figured I was bound to get some referrals as well.

My wife and I had no money of any significance, and we gave up spending on anything but necessi-ties like food. We both remember the excitement of seeing state and local government checks hit our mailbox from the cases I had completed. Our first major purchase after I got paid was a $200.00 chiminea for our backyard. One would have thought we built an in-ground pool. That chiminea represented a comeback. I was finally on the road to mental and financial stability and my wife could breathe a sigh of relief at seeing her husband fulfilling his role as the principal breadwinner.

Change is usually never easy even when one carefully plans for it, but the sort of change I experienced once my ex-wife left was forced upon me. I am only now starting to come to terms with my new life. But to be clear, change and its concomitant anxiety can affect everyone, including children and pets. I do not think my children ever fully realized how the separation and divorce would affect them, even though they were grown and out of the nest when it occurred. No longer would we take a vacation as a complete family unit or all share a holiday together. No longer would they make one call and reach both of their parents.

My dog, Oscar, has not been spared the change and resulting anxiety. Oscar is a Golden Retriever, a breed known to be docile, and yet he snaps and snarls at other dogs who dare to enter the invisible zone of protection he encases around me. He now barely leaves my side and cries as I enter the home in the afternoons because he missed me. This dog has experienced every feeling I have. I have tried my best to pay him extra special attention, but I know he felt as lonely as I did.

He was used to having a family to take him on walks around the neighborhood, to let him loose at the dog park, or to rub his belly at night. Many days, I felt completely drained and filled with overwhelming emotion and anxiety. At those times, he never failed to sense those things and curl up next to me just to let me know he loved me. I count my dog as being one of my best friends. He is certainly the most loyal.

I could write separately just about domestic pets, but I think by now, most people are keenly aware of their benefits. They are brought in to cheer up the infirm. They can be emotional support pets to those with emotional disorders and are used as seeing-eye dogs to navigate for the blind. Pets are amazing, and we are blessed to live in a world inhabited by them as opposed to the opposite.

In my line of work as a criminal defense attorney, the cases I always dreaded most involved animals and children. I dreaded them because I know that though the Constitution provides the cloak of innocence around every defendant, as a practical matter, when it comes to children and animals, the presumption of innocence shifts to a presumption of guilt. A defendant charged with a crime against an animal or a child better be prepared to prove his innocence rather than the other way around.

Change affects people in different ways. Some people welcome change and view it as a fresh start. Others, like me, stick with routines to purposely avoid change. For example, I will eat at the same restaurants on the same days and order the same food because once I get accustomed to something, I will not upset the apple cart.

CHAPTER 7
NOT TRIGGER HAPPY

As referenced in the preceding chapter, my ex-wife and my daughter were attending the wedding of my daughter's childhood friend. My daughter was in the bridal party and my ex-wife had come down from her new home in New York to attend because, like the rest of us, we had known the bride-to-be since she was a toddler.

A couple of weeks before the wedding, I believe I had battled the Omicron variant of Covid-19. Truth be told, I was never tested, but I had all the hallmarks of the variant. I elected not to get tested for two reasons: even if I were positive, the treatment would include three things: rest, fluids, and quarantine, something I did not need to make a copay to be told.

Second, I felt so sick I did not relish waiting three hours in a waiting room only to be told to do those three things. So I drank fluids, rested, tried to eat, and self-quarantined. What I did not expect was the grim reaper of Covid was lurking around the corner, waiting to pounce after my recovery was complete. I later learned this condition that still confounds doctors worldwide is known synonymously as Post-Covid or Long-Haul-Covid (which I will refer to henceforth as LHC).

LHC was the term used to describe the remnants of Covid that remain in different organs of the body and that manifests itself in several ways from sleep disorders and loss of appetite to neurological disorders including brain fog and, most notably, anxiety and depression. Unfortunately, the confluence of several factors ("triggers") exacerbated the onset of LHC, which, up to that point, had gone unnoticed by me.

This was not unusual because the scientific community had at least reached a consensus that LHC typically manifested roughly one week after recovery. That was the precise timing of the wedding. Scientists also believed LHC could last weeks, months, or even up to a year, although there is no consensus. Exactly the role LHC played in my sudden meltdown I will never know, but I feel certain it played a part because the sudden and persistent onslaught of anxiety and depression struck suddenly and with a vengeance.

I was not vaccinated then, and I remain unvaccinated. Call me a conspiracy theorist, but I believe a vaccine of this type rushed through the laboratory by Big Pharma at warp speed with no human testing, no control group, and no way of ascertaining its efficacy was not something I should take. Based on some of the side effects observable and verifiable in the Vaccine Adverse Event Reporting System ("VAERS") run by the Department of Health and Human Services, I think I made a wise choice.

I learned there are no accurate tests to determine whether one has LHC. I was at a wedding with my ex-wife whom I had not seen for a few months and we were, by all outward appearances, holding ourselves out as a couple. But I was triggered.

I was attending a celebratory function in which they repeatedly stated that two newlyweds shall remain together until death they should part. I was standing next to a woman who was divorcing me while the newlyweds were introduced for the first time as husband and wife. This caused a massive trigger. A trigger can be a certain smell, music, an activity, or almost anything that transports someone to another place. We are familiar with certain songs that instantly remind us of moments in time.

I was mentally transported back in time to the Hotel Thayer at West Point, where my wife and I had one of the most memorable celebrations anyone can recall. For years, our wedding reception was held as the standard bearer for what a wedding reception should be. We had incredible food and all the top shelf alcohol one cared to imbibe. Everyone was happy and drunk and vice versa. Growing up in North Carolina, I was more accustomed to the obligatory non-alcoholic fruit punch and cake in the church reception hall.

My mind transported me back to 1990; only what were once happy memories now wreaked havoc on my psyche. This wedding—this ceremonious occasion—did just that to me. I watched as the newlyweds not only danced to their wedding song but invited other couples to join. My wife and I never danced, but stood as silent spectators.

In a slow regression, my mind took me back thirty-one years to a time when I was doing the very same things with my wife. Now the occasion was not ceremonious, but confusing. I was unwittingly being mind-fucked, a term I think adequately describes the psychological effect events can have on one's mind following a trigger.

This was the granddaddy of all triggers. Call it post-traumatic stress disorder or something else, all I know is the onslaught of LHC and this massive trigger fucked my mind so hard it left me doing a one year walk of shame.

I had no conscious idea about the truly destructive force of triggers and I believe my feelings were attributable to LHC. I was referred by a friend to a doctor in Richmond who specializes in LHC. Again, little was known then or now about LHC. The doctor met me privately at her home and prescribed ivermectin, a routine therapeutic medication that unfortunately became the tip of the controversial and conspiratorial spear of Covid relief. That was the real reason we secretly met at her home.

I desperately treated myself with other home remedies too, basically anything the internet suggested might help. I still have a hefty supply of vitamins of every type, including tryptophan, magnesium, and aspergillum. If the internet suggested certain supplements might help, I tried them. Whether LHC truly contributed to my condition or whether I had simply been subjected to a relentless mind fuck is irrelevant. I felt like a 20-megaton trigger had been dropped on me that no Geiger counter could measure.

I was being bombarded with triggers and the biggest one occurred just after the wedding was over when my wife reminded me it was time to pay up. She was *entitled* to her equitable share of one of our houses—a house she never wanted from the start. This was a four-bedroom ranch in Chesapeake, VA. I bought it with the intention of converting it into my new law office. It was in a prime location directly across from City Hall and a short walk from the courthouses. Anyone going to or coming from court would have to pass by this house/office.

The conversion from a residential house to an office required me to, among other things, rezone the property from residential to commercial, to cut down most of the trees, to pave a parking lot, and to remodel the interior. The premise was sound, but the timing was poor. All the upfront expenses required may have been manageable, but my son was about to begin college and I needed money to pay for his tuition, room, and board, etc. I tabled my plan to convert the house to my office and opted instead to rent it.

In any event, my life seemed extremely content leading up to the triggers. I had few noticeable signs of anxiety or depression, and I was functioning at a high level. Looking back now, I recognize the triggers were hitting me from all sides. In what seemed like an instant, triggers were bringing me to one of the lowest points of my life. As previously discussed, I was obsessed with money out of the irrational fear of figuratively going back to that broken down trailer. I voraciously saved as much money as I could because I wanted to retire sooner rather than later and wanted to maintain my current lifestyle.

During the time I was triggered, I also became acutely aware that my business had all but come to an end. The phones were simply not ringing, and I had been asleep at the switch, completely consumed by the triggers and unaware of my cash flow until it had depleted. The business pipeline valve sealed shut, and I panicked.

I checked my website and did a search engine search and realized my phone had not been ringing because my placement had dropped off the first page. If I learned anything over the years, it is that people will generally look no further than the first few search result listings. After that, one may as well have no internet presence at all.

At the same time, I saw my wife stealing what I had without the means to support myself. Again, I was mind-fucked into believing we were nearing the apocalypse—the end times. We had a pandemic, a massive economic decline, out-of-control inflation, soaring gasoline prices, an economic recession, and my investment portfolio value was slashed in half. In the aggregate, this was a catastrophe of biblical proportions and none of that was seemingly considered by my ex-wife, as I was expected to pay her a marital entitlement. I felt I was being forced into indentured servitude for seven more years to pay spousal support. My job was so stressful that I could not imagine doing it for seven more years. Though the job had treated me well financially, it had taken a physical and emotional toll on me.

I can think of only three times I was triggered or potentially triggered. The first was after my younger brother committed suicide in 1988 and I joined the Coast Guard in 1989. During training, I went to the shooting range to test-fire the M16 rifle. Every time I heard a shot ring out, I thought of my brother and I could hear his gun. I could not focus and when it came time to test, I failed miserably.

At times during my shooting qualification test, my eyes glazed over, making the target nearly impossible to see. Other times I pointed the barrel of the rifle downrange toward the target without really aiming and just pulled the trigger. I did not care if I hit the target or not. Not surprisingly, I didn't even qualify for Marksman, the lowest level qualification. A few years later, when I was in a much better emotional state, I tested again and qualified as an Expert Marksman, the highest level qualification.

Second, while attending Catholic Mass alone and flipping through the missal, I saw that one of the musical selections included *On Eagles Wings*, a composition sung at my wedding. I was expecting a trigger and, perhaps because I was expecting it and had time to prepare, it did not happen. I also think my head was in a slightly better place where every little thing that could be a trigger fizzles out and has minimal to no effect.

I say minimal only because though I was not triggered, per se, I was eager to see that song end. But my feeling was and still is, why tempt fate? If a potential trigger can be avoided, avoid it. If it cannot be avoided or if you simply choose to test yourself to determine the state of your mental health, I see nothing wrong with that approach either if you envision the best outcome but are prepared for the worst.

Thirdly, when September 11, 2001 occurred, an all-call went out to all lawyers who could volunteer to assist family members prepare affidavits regarding their loved ones. In 2001, under New York law, if a person went missing, family members were required to wait one year before their loved one could be presumed dead. Only then could the family collect from a life insurance policy. The thought was that after a year it was a safe enough bet the person was deceased.

On September 11, 2001, the world watched as the twin towers of the World Trade Center (WTC) collapsed. It seemed obvious to anyone that no one could survive the free-fall of tons of steel and concrete pulverized during its 102-story descent. Accordingly, the law was changed to allow families to collect immediately from anyone thought to be in the WTC. The only requirement was they had to answer questions in an affidavit specifically stating where their family members worked within the WTC and why they believed they had been at work in the WTC on September 11th. I was specifically tasked with helping the families of the first responders complete their affidavits.

This was already an emotional time for the entire country, let alone these families, but to complete the affidavit was an acknowledgment that their loved ones were dead even though a search and rescue/recovery operation was still underway. Often family members started out strong and about halfway through the Q&A period of the affidavit, they broke down and could proceed no further.

September 11, 2001, was depressing for a lot of people. It also exposed our national vulnerabilities and changed the way our nation conducts business. During that time, we saw stock markets plummet and airline traffic halted. The Department of Homeland Security was created, which included federalizing the passenger screening process by the newly formed Transportation Security Administration and the USA Patriot Act was passed.

Life in America was inalterably changed or abolished, along with many of the protections given to us by the Constitution, all in the name of protecting the homeland. I have since read extensively about the persons truly responsible for the 9/11 attacks and just to jump to the punchline, it was not Osama Bin Laden or a small cadre of Islamic Extremists armed with box cutters (essentially Exacto knives, but this is a deeper subject for a different book).

For at least five years after September 11, 2001, I could not watch any news coverage on the anniversary of 9/11. Those emotional memories were etched into my psyche and remembering the look, feel, and smell of 9/11 came flooding back to me each time I saw a replay of those towers falling and people walking uptown on 5th Avenue, their bodies covered in ashes from head to toe.

As I mentioned in the *Introduction*, I had already provided so much as a father and as a husband that I questioned myself about why I was still shaving years off my life to do something I no longer needed or wanted to do. Except now I had obligated myself to pay monthly spousal support to a woman who was no longer going to be a part of my life.

I resented the hell out of it. I believed I had given her more money than she would have had if she saved every penny from the beginning of time. I felt I was being punished for my success. From a macro point of view, I wondered how I was going to pay her entitlement when the world's economy appeared to be blowing up. From a micro perspective, the business I spent many years fostering was imploding. I could not see a pathway forward.

The public has no sense of the burden lawyers carry daily, at least those lawyers who really care about the well-being of their clients and are not only in it for the money. Meteorologists can be wrong ninety percent of the time and still maintain employment. Lawyers must be right 100% of the time.

There is no room for error, especially for a criminal litigator. I would often say the only thing standing between my clients and prison was me. Sometimes I told people if I failed to bring my *A-game,* someone was going to prison. If prosecutors lose a case, no one goes to prison. On the other hand, criminal defense lawyers have an immense responsibility to construct a defense in many indefensible situations with clients who often have unrealistic expectations.

Don't do the crime if you can't do the time sounds catchy, but it is not something to which most clients ascribe. I have seen first-hand how many well-intentioned people commit subsequent crimes because the first crime was not impressionable enough for them. They hired an attorney who got them out of trouble and they felt invincible. Obviously, many people make the calculated, although unwise, decision to carry out often unthinkable crimes and expect the lawyer to swoop in on his white horse to save the day.

Likewise, in divorce cases, typically one spouse wants to keep one hundred percent of the marital assets while the opposing spouse wants one hundred percent. Although this is parametrically impossible, clients refuse to concede and lawyers are left to win an unwinnable battle. The hired-gun-win-at-any-cost mentality is prevalent among lawyers, consequently, they find themselves pitted against other lawyers all in the name of winning the skirmish du jour. It was always my belief that lawyers should try to solve problems, not create them, but when one is getting paid significantly to carry out his client's wishes, that philosophy gets quickly cast aside.

The enormous pressures faced by lawyers daily have created a subculture of very stressed-out, burned-out individuals who must at least meet and often exceed their clients' expectations. Lawyering is like playing high stakes poker where the winner takes all and whose stock-in-trade soars while the loser reaps little qualitative or quantitative prospective rewards because his reputation for winning gets sullied even though he did the best he could with the facts he was dealt.

One negative review can mean the difference between success and failure, especially for the sole practitioner. Consequently, a high incidence of drug use, alcoholism, depression and even suicide is prevalent among lawyers. For this reason, the Virginia State Bar (VSB) established a program called the Virginia Judges and Lawyers Assistance Program (VJLAP), formerly known as Virginia Lawyers Helping Lawyers.

VJLAP is the VSB's attempt to help lawyers in crisis. It is a confidential hotline where lawyers can get advice and help from other lawyers. During my struggles, I contacted them and they provided no help to me, apart from asking me how I was doing. If I could give the VJLAP one piece of advice, it would be to help lawyers, not only provide lip-service. An occasional check-in phone call or email is woefully inadequate.

I recall a lawyer coming to me once because he was overwhelmed and distraught. He was new to the practice of law and took on too many cases. I saw he was decompensating. He could not handle the pressure. I still fail to understand how lawyers fresh out of law school are so willing to hang their shingles and take on complex legal cases with no practical experience. Perhaps the allure of money is too great, or maybe they just could not find employment within an established firm. Who knows?

This was the mistake my colleague made. He sat in my office, and I could plainly see he had the one-thousand-yard stare I experienced. I told him not to worry, I would fix his problems. I called many of his clients and, without going into any details, simply told them he had a serious medical condition and could not continue working on their cases. To my surprise, everyone voiced sincere concern and unhesitatingly said no problem; they would find another lawyer. I solved his problems that day. He has been forever grateful I did what needed to be done at that moment.

At a minimum, I think VJLAP should do that much —meet with the attorney having a mental health crisis and see what they can do to mitigate that crisis, at least with respect to the lawyer's caseload. Don't expect a lawyer in crisis to meet with you and, above all, don't believe the lawyer if he tells you he'll be fine. After all, he called you for a reason. Anyway, the lawyer I helped has since gone on to do great things in his profession and has a thriving practice, but for that moment in time, he needed to be relieved of the immense pressure he was feeling.

At times during my divorce, my confidence had been blown, and I felt I could not adequately represent myself, let alone anyone else. With every passing day, my anxiety grew worse as I approached deadlines for motions and the biggest trial I had taken on for many years. I wondered how I would do and whether I would find myself in full-blown panic mode when the time arrived.

Often, I had to talk myself out of bed to fulfill obligations. Oddly enough, new business was both a blessing and a curse. On the one hand, I needed new business as a revenue source. On the other hand, new business represented future stress and anxiety and the continuation of a law practice I was not at all sure I wanted to do and was mentally prepared to handle.

My confidence was brought to heel during a simple assault criminal case in which I was massively triggered while conducting my cross-examination. The female complainant had accused my male client of purposely throwing an object at her that, although didn't strike her, was thrown in a *rude, angry, vengeful* manner, intending to make contact. After she testified on direct examination, it was my job to destroy her credibility.

During cross-examination, lawyers are allowed to ask leading questions. Leading questions are generally thought to be those that require a *yes* or *no* answer or suggest a specific answer. For example, "You never told anyone about the assault, did you? You testified today to XYZ, but you never stated that in your written complaint, did you? On the date of the offense, you were wearing a blue shirt, correct?"

The *victim* simply refused to give me a straightforward answer to my questions. Whenever she answered, she tried doing so in a narrative. She simply refused to answer yes or no without further commentary. After a short period of trying to get her to answer, I lost my composure and started yelling at her to answer my questions. Every time she tried to dance around the question, I unloaded on her.

Here was a woman who, for that moment, was a proxy for my ex-wife and I was not letting her off the hook. Finally, the bailiff yelled *order in the court* and I calmed down. My client was acquitted of the charge and was happy with both my performance and the outcome of the trial, but it was not my finest hour. The following day, I apologized to the bailiff, and I cryptically told him why it happened. He was understanding and not at all judgmental. He simply said, *no big deal; it happens.*

As apocalyptic as I saw my life following the trigger, I later looked for little things for encouragement. I dropped about twenty pounds at the height of my mental meltdown, mostly because I had no appetite. My weight had been a steady 221, and I got down to what for me was a skinny 201. For the longest time I hovered around 207-208 pounds and no matter what I did, I could not seem to break through that barrier. Once I finally saw my weight creep up around the 215 range, I knew I was on the mend.

I also strangely looked at gas prices as a positive sign of my recovery. Recall that the lack of business (meaning money) and soaring gas prices were major contributors to my massive anxiety. As strange as this may sound, every time I passed a gas station and saw that prices had dropped, even if only by a few cents, I found myself a little more gleeful.

Isaac Newton's Third Law of Motion posits that, for every action, there is an equal but opposite reaction. This might well explain why the needle on my positivity continuum moved up with every minimal price drop in gasoline. The cost of gasoline became a strange sort of gauge of my mental fitness.

I found myself needing to relax more than ever. I craved my time of relaxation and anything or anyone who interrupted my tranquility usually felt my wrath. I am not proud of that, but my reaction only solidified the thought that this was my time. This was the chance for me to focus on myself alone. I did everything I could do for everyone else and now was the time for me to become more selfcentered. But it seemed like relaxation was hard to find, as every little thing took on a life of its own. My mind was exhausted.

One night, a smoke alarm started chirping, and I attempted to change the batteries, only to have the alarm continue to chirp. I tried everything I knew to stop it, but the sound was literally driving me insane. There was no way I was going to relax with a near 20,000 hertz ear-piercing chirp intermittently disturbing me. I finally ripped the alarm off the wall and yet it continued to chirp. I slept with my noise canceling headphones on my head and listened to relaxation music.

The piercing alarm penetrated through my headphones until I finally gave up and spent the rest of the night trying to fall asleep outdoors on the chaise lounge. I was emotionally and physically exhausted. As the sun appeared, I made a desperate call to the electrician who came out after I was gone.

It turned out the smoke alarm was never chirping; it was the carbon monoxide alarm. The sound had ricocheted around the hallway, so it sounded as if it was coming from the smoke alarm. It turned out all I had to do to stop the chirping was to change the batteries in my CO_2 alarm or unplug it. I felt somewhat vindicated, and frankly less idiotic after the electrician told me he too had a difficult time understanding why the chirping was so persistent.

The biggest thing I could do to help myself relax was not to speak with my wife. We disagreed on many aspects of our settlement, leading to both of us talking to each other with hostility. The vitriol in her voice reminded me of the time her father had come to my house and said God-awful things to me before I moved to Virginia. Every little thing triggered me. Looking back, I was out of control. She did not deserve my vitriol, but at that moment in time, I cared about nothing or no one.

CHAPTER 8
AGREE TO DISAGREE

My wife and I had arrived at an amicable property settlement agreement. I did all the initial work on it and handed it over to her. I tried my best to be civil throughout the process, but it was difficult. She worked as my secretary for many years and knew the ins and outs of divorce and what she was *entitled* to.

Anytime I heard her utter the word entitlement, my skin crawled. I thought about where she was when I was working a full-time job in the Coast Guard and going to law school at night. Where was she, besides minding the children, when I spent every waking moment studying for the New York State Bar exam?

Before you take exception to that, I am extremely grateful to her for caring for our children. I never had to worry about their well-being. She taught them many things and prepared them both for preschool and beyond. My children are incredibly confident and well-adjusted because of her. I readily concede all of that.

I suppose my position was they were her children too, so those tasks had to be far more enjoyable than writing legal papers, reading legal opinions, and studying. But none of those things mattered. She felt entitled to fifty percent of our assets and whatever sacrifices I made and stress I endured acquiring those assets were irrelevant. Whether I was right or wrong for having those feelings did not matter to me. My feelings were my feelings.

I had the templates stored on my computer hard drive at work for everything relating to divorce, and I told her we did not need any other lawyers to get involved. I would take care of everything. I still believed she was being unfair to me, but I agreed to her demands and I typed the agreement. We were civil for most of the time, but occasionally she said I was too combative, and she felt she needed to get her own attorney.

The thing I knew was I did not need or want another attorney telling me what I had to do with my things. I responded by telling her if she got her own attorney and I received anything from them, I was going to go to the attorney's office with papers in hand and tear those papers into tiny pieces and throw them all over the floor. I totally did not care. A judge could order me to jail at that point. It mattered not to me. If my wife wanted to send the father of her children, the man who had provided her a great life, to jail, so be it. She said I was being completely unfair to her. That angered me even more. But eventually we agreed on the division of assets, and we memorialized it all in a property and settlement agreement.

I was not ecstatic about it, but I knew I had accomplished the one thing that mattered most to me—I would be able to look straight into my children's eyes and say I had done right by their mother. I was trying to set a good example for them, even if it meant getting a huge financial haircut.

Everything between the two of us seemed okay for a time. We had a signed agreement I was willing to live with and we had no real reason to speak with one another. Then one day she called me crying. She said I had treated her unfairly, and she felt she should get more spousal support and for a longer duration.

Always a sucker for emotion, I agreed right away without even thinking about what it meant for me. I had agreed to revise our earlier proposal and later typed the revisions to spousal support, and we re-executed that part of the agreement and supplanted it for the original version. We had agreed only to disagree.

I was not terribly concerned about the newer, longer, and more robust agreement because my mind was clear at that moment. The agreement also called for me to buy out her equity stake of the marital home, the investment house on Cedar Road, and for us to co-own the beach house. I was to change the deed on the beach house to joint-tenancy with right of survivorship.

The original plan was for us to maintain ownership of the beach house and run it as a business, carving out a few weeks for our personal use. Property values were soaring and Cape Charles, VA, as a destination, was growing ever more popular. We agreed that if I died first, she would get one hundred percent of the property and if she died first, I would. This once-in-my-lifetime home was something I was most proud of. I had literally put my heart and soul into it. I wanted to hand it down to children someday and, in the interim, allow them to vacation there with their families.

I agreed to continue managing the property as a vacation rental property through Airbnb and Vrbo. However, if any repairs needed to be made, it would be my responsibility to arrange for them. Although we jointly owned the property, because of my proximity to the house, the cleaning staff always informed me of anything that was stained, damaged, or out of place. I received photos of every juice-box stain on the carpet, every utensil that wasn't cleaned and properly stowed, every scratch on every appliance, and every piece of furniture that was ajar.

The cleaning crew was a mother and daughter combo, and they were extremely professional and thorough. I also consider them friends. But I just could not take the phone calls anymore. I was usually polite with the cleaners, but I was tired of hearing about the problems with that house. I lost my temper more than once and I finally told them to start discussing the problems with my wife. I needed to distance myself from the issues for my own sanity.

That house became a sore subject for me in many ways. Whenever I visited, it no longer brought me joy. It only brought me heartache because I was reminded this had been our family's vacation home. We spent nearly every weekend there with the children during quarantine. The very last time I had been there, the house was filled with the sounds of my family. Now it was merely a sarcophagus.

Twice I took women to the house for a quick overnight getaway. Little did I realize I would be triggered during that process. The first woman slept in a separate bedroom because I was not feeling amorous and the second never even made it that far. I began feeling sick to my stomach as soon as we arrived at Cape Charles, and we drove back across the Chesapeake Bay Bridge Tunnel to Virginia Beach by 9:00 p.m.

When I was massively triggered around the time of the wedding, the earlier revisions to our agreement, at least with respect to keeping the beach house, went out with the tide. I had to find an escape route for the spousal support that bound my life and career. In a moment of a massive panic attack, I remember texting my ex-wife only two words: *sell everything* and we did. Later, as I regained more control over my life, I regretted that decision.

I truly loved that house and saw it as not only as a place of complete respite, but also as a fantastic investment. That house was a three-story home with decks overlooking the Chesapeake Bay and marina. It was incredibly gorgeous, and a dream come true for me. It really epitomized my success. However, selling it was the only decision I felt capable of making during my panic phase.

I understand how a stockbroker must feel when markets plummet and he is trying to offload equities as quickly as possible. I have heard about brokers taking their own lives during such stressful times, some reportedly jumped out of windows to their deaths. The feeling of panic and massive burning anxiety overtakes any sense of reality. Rational thinking skills can become obliterated.

CHAPTER 9
GUMMIES FOR DUMMIES

I heard CBD gummies were all the rage. Many swear gummies will help take off the edge of anxiety. I was desperate to find something—anything—that would make me feel better, make me feel *normal* again, and heard all I needed to hear. I knew I had what was projected to be a two-week jury trial on the horizon and needed to get myself back in fighting shape.

I will never forget going to the tobacco and vape shop one Friday morning and asking the young man behind the counter about gummies. Outwardly, he was the perfect person to run that store. His stereotypical mannerism and appearance said he had a wealth of experience using gummy worms and I suspected a lot more. I explained I really needed to relax and was told he had just the thing. I specifically mentioned CBD gummies, but either he didn't hear me or willfully ignored me. He said, *I have something special for you* as he handed me a bag of sours. I admit I didn't look carefully at the bag. I only recall his saying to go easy if I had no experience with them.

He suggested I bite off one-twelfth of a gummy worm to start, not one-tenth, but one-twelfth. My first thought was, can we round that down a bit? But rather than break out a ruler, I decided to just open the bag. I ripped open the top of the bag and pulled out one tasty sour invertebrate, pinched off what I believed to be one-twelfth, and swallowed it whole. He said give it about an hour, and I would feel very relaxed. I teemed with excitement. Had I finally found the one elixir to set my mind at ease, reduce my anxiety, and prepare me for the jury trial that was all-encompassing my mind? Only time would tell.

Keeping a close monitor on my wristwatch, I waited the full hour, but to my dismay, I felt nothing. I then made a command decision to take a heftier bite, this time ingesting the equivalent of one-half a gummy. No problem, I thought.

I had scheduled a meeting with two of the Commonwealth's Attorneys at 3:00 p.m. that Friday. With the slowdown in work and not wanting to wait around all afternoon, I texted the lead prosecutor and told him my doctor had a cancellation and I needed to reschedule the meeting for the following week. None of that was true, but I wanted out. He quickly replied he was on vacation the following week but had availability immediately and asked if I could make it. Feeling nothing from the gummies, I texted *sure*.

I drove over to the Commonwealth's Attorney's office and went inside. I told the receptionist about the meeting and sat on a nearby couch. The lead prosecutor and his assistant walked out and advised they had forgotten about another meeting with detectives and asked whether I would mind sitting for about a half hour. Naturally I agreed. Once their meeting was over, the lead prosecutor asked me to follow him to his office. I still felt little to nothing from the gummies until I stood up. At that point, my thoughts were drawn to one thing: *Holy Shit! What have I done?*

I was about to hear new evidence in a murder case in which I represented the defendant and I was higher than Mount Everest. My legs were wobbly and my gate was staggered. I had no experience with any drugs except for once circa 1986. I met a girl who worked at KFC. We hit it off and agreed to go out.

I was to pick her up at her apartment, but before leaving, she pulled out a bong. She asked if I wanted to smoke pot. I had never smoked pot, but respected its power. I was keenly aware of three things that were popular opinions: pot gets you high, pot makes you hungry, and pot makes a girl horny. Of course, I agreed without hesitation. We never left her apartment that night and, after that, I had empirical evidence to support all three popular opinions.

Getting back to my meeting—I found myself slouched in the chair, listening to the exuberance of the prosecutors as they went through their evidence in painstaking detail. To them, they had my guy dead to rights. My only questions to them at that very moment were *who is alleged to have killed whom* and *with what?*

I obviously already knew the answers when I was sober, but I was high and barely knew my own name. I mainly focused on repeating the information they had just given me, as if they did not know. I did my best to comprehend and took some barely legible notes. At that moment, all I could think about was my escape route. I thought about how I was going to get out of there without raising suspicions. I finally made the excuse that I needed to get to my fake doctor's appointment.

Whew! The meeting was over and I survived. As normal protocol dictated, I was escorted out of the office by one of the prosecutors. If awards were given for acting, I deserved both the Golden Globe and the Oscar, but if I had to take a field sobriety test, I would have failed miserably. Once back in my car, I was able to orient myself for the short drive home. The worst was yet to come.

I made it home safely and promptly found haven in the security of my bed. Shortly after, I found myself staring at the ceiling, wondering what the hell was happening to me. The more I wondered about whether I was dying, the more I felt the onset of anxiety.

I experienced a brain freeze-type sensation, only an order of magnitude greater. Most people have probably felt that indescribable but extremely painful feeling in their heads whenever they drink a frozen drink too fast. It causes dire pain. I do not know how it feels to have a stroke, but I suspect the sharp sensation in my head was at least as bad.

I was writhing in pain and confusion. The feeling reminded me of the time I took Seroquel.

I could not concentrate and the more I attempted to do so, the more the power of the gummies and concomitant anxiety pulled me right back. I needed to do something and do it fast. My thoughts immediately went to the gym. If I could only ride the lifecycle, I thought, I could work that mess out of my system.

I clumsily dressed out in workout attire and drove to the gym, still writhing in pain from the *brain freeze*. I made a beeline for the lifecycle and began riding the bike as if my life depended on it and for what seemed like an eternity. That was Plan A: ride the lifecycle and sweat it out. I rode a long time and with vengeance, or so I thought. After what seemed like ten or fifteen minutes, imagine my horror when I looked down at the machine and saw I had only been riding for about two minutes.

At that very moment, I felt trapped in an episode of the *Twilight Zone*. It was the most bizarre thing I had ever encountered. I then decided to switch to Plan B—get into the dry sauna and sweat it out. Normally, I begin sweating in the sauna within thirty seconds or so. But this time was different. I was sitting in the sauna for eight minutes, but did not sweat a single drop. My skin was ice cold to the touch. I panicked. Something was seriously wrong with me, and I knew I needed to get out. I had the fortitude to text my doctor on his personal cell-phone and the following is the exact text message exchange:

Friday, June 24th 4:04 p.m.

Me: *Not sure if this means anything, but I can't sweat. I got out of the sauna and my skin is cold.*

Dr: *Not sure.*

Me: *No sweating.*

Dr: *Maybe fever coming on?*

Me: *I don't think so.*

Dr: *Keep an eye on it.*

Me: *I will.*

Dr: *Good.*

That was the end of that. I decided the best thing for me to do at that moment was to go home again and try to sleep it off. I left the gym and attempted to sleep, but the pain and anxiety were just too great. I decided to re-execute Plans A and B, and I did so like a man on a mission.

I returned to the gym a second time and was a little more relieved when my skin began to shed a few beads of sweat. Not much, but I was making progress. I really wanted to do a full-blown workout but felt incapable.

I left the gym for the second time, slightly more relieved that maybe the worst was over. Once I left the gym, I got the munchies and went to a local delicatessen to eat. I was now ready to return to the gym a third time to do what I initially tried to do.

You may be starting to see now why I gave the gym honorable mention in my *Introduction*. Not only was it healthy, but it was something for me to do to occupy my mind, body, and soul. If an idle mind is the devil's workshop, I was not about to turn mine into *This Old House*.

Only after returning home the third time and reading the bag did I realize I had not taken CBD, but rather a bag containing 3,800 milligrams of THC. My foray into the world of THC and CBD gummies came to an abrupt end that Friday. Although this story is funny to tell in retrospect, at the time, it was the most terrifying ordeal I had ever experienced.

I had no idea what was happening to me and had excruciating and persistent pain and anxiety. I finally felt something pop inside my head that day, as if a pressure valve had exploded. I was convinced I had some sort of brain aneurysm, but I felt paralyzed to do anything about it. I was resigned to the fact that Friday, June 24, 2022, would be my last day on earth and I laid in bed, having fully accepted my fate.

CHAPTER 10
NUN NADA ZILCH

Whenever my marriage abruptly ended, I tried to understand who I was and what I was meant to do, hence the title of this book—*Identity Crisis*. Faith had gotten me through so many of my trying times in the past and, once again, I called on God to help. I incessantly prayed, hoping for a miracle.

When things seemed to stall somewhat, my mind was drawn to my priest. After all, who is better to be the intermediary between God and me but my priest? It had worked for me in the past, and there was no reason to think it wouldn't work again.

I believe in the power of prayer and absolution, and my priest was one who could provide both. In

1990, during the period of Pre-Cana, which is a prerequisite for all Catholic weddings, I had the privilege of absorbing the profound wisdom of a priest, Father Jack. The teachings and insights of Father Jack, a man of immense spirituality, have remained etched in my memory till this very day.

Father Jack not only guided us through Pre-Cana, but also officiated at our wedding ceremony. Despite his towering height of approximately six feet and six inches, he exuded a gentle and approachable demeanor. He was truly a remarkable man, a gentle giant in every sense of the word.

Prayer is one of those things I treated like reading. I would get addicted to reading at various times and read voraciously, sometimes two or three books at a time. I could be like the Forrest Gump of reading. But like Forrest who ran day-in and day out and then abruptly stopping, I could go from a one to three book a day habit to quitting cold turkey. Unfortunately, I would often say three or four prayers a day every day especially when I needed God's help, but then stop suddenly as soon as the crisis averted. I'm not proud of that but it's the truth.

In the beginning, I felt I could not rely on my own prayers as if I did not have the qualifications or charisma to be my own spokesman. I felt I needed assistance from someone more connected. That person was my priest.

In the early stages of our marital troubles, I suggested to my wife we go to speak with our priest. I was hoping, like Father Jack, we would come away with a renewed sense of commitment to each other. My wife was adamantly opposed to that suggestion. She was far more committed to attending Mass than I was, and she thought divulging our innermost marital secrets to our priest would be far too embarrassing.

My wife did not know until much later I had already spoken to our priest and came away feeling like my soul had been healed. I had a newfound sense of purpose to strengthen and fortify our marriage. Had she known about my clandestine meeting, she would have been mortified. I think she thought she could never show her face around the parish again after I confided in our parish Father. But it was one of the most memorable things I did.

I recall vividly walking into the parish office in tears, hoping Father was around to listen and pray over me. I was desperate to see him. Feeling depressed, I turned to the word of God. The first question I was asked (and rightfully, I suppose) was whether I had an appointment to see Father. I did not. But seeing the distress on my face, the woman in the business office spoke with Father and asked him if he would see me. He agreed.

It did not take long before I began weeping like a child before Father. Here I was a grown man, sixty years old, clamoring for hope, and he did not disappoint. I came away from our brief encounter with a revitalized spirit and a renewed sense of purpose. He placed his hands on my head exactly like Father Jack had done thirty-one years prior during our wedding nuptials. I felt a power permeate my head and a force that restored my confidence and renewed the faith that I could and would survive during the most tempestuous period of my life.

My first meeting with Father had such healing qualities that when I felt I needed that sort of intersession again, I wasted no time in seeking Father's prayerful help. Most people know the stages of grief as denial, anger, bargaining, depression, and acceptance. I maneuvered easily in the denial phase. I met a few women online and acted as though nothing phased me.

I briefly went through the anger phase with my wife. After all, though I was not the perfect husband, I had given her a great life, at least material-istically. I cannot say I went through any sort of bargaining phase that I assume means if the pain only goes away, I promise to be a better man. But once the depression finally hit me, it leveled me like a tsunami. By the time it became apparent, I was unable to seek refuge at the time it struck. I was unprepared for its relentless force and dev-astation.

Once fully engulfed in the depression stage of grief, I again felt impelled to speak with Father. His healing hands were what I thought I needed. Up to this point, I had been relegated to reading the daily scripture and prayers from the Holy Bible app.

If you ever wondered whether we are a capitalist society, you need only install the Holy Bible app. Before getting to the scripture and prayers, I had to frustratingly watch the obligatory commercials for Candy Crush and other annoying advertisements when all I really wanted was to read words of in-spiration and prayer.

I once again found myself standing in the business office of my parish. I never knew when grief and hopelessness would overwhelm me, so I did not have the foresight to make an appointment. I was incredibly distraught. Not only had depression taken hold of me, but now it had morphed into uncontrollable anxiety. I was in emotional free fall.

Sadness was visibly apparent as I once again asked to speak to Father. I was told he was busy and could not speak to me. I understand priests have many commitments from visiting the infirm to taking Eucharist to the homebound to presiding over funerals and the like, so I did not make much fuss. I did the next best thing and asked whether I could go into the Church Nave to pray because the private chapel was being used for a webcast of the Rosary. The private chapel was once my favorite place to go, but when Covid hit, the chapel was transformed into a makeshift internet broadcast studio.

I prayed aloud, pouring out my soul to God and asking him to take away my heartache and pain. These things were simply too excruciating for me to bear alone. After some period, I moved toward the exit of the office with tear trails on my face, coming down in all directions, making my face look like a ski resort map with each tear stream representing a downhill trail from the summit.

My depression, anxiety, grief, angst, and sorrow were obvious. Yet, the only thing anyone asked was whether I was okay. Of course, I said I was. I was not about to say, N*o, I am thinking of commit-ting suicide* (a thought I often had). Without skip-ping a beat, my response said in a low, somber tone while wiping the tears away from my eyes was, *I am okay*. It was obvious I was not.

I often wonder if it would have mattered to anyone if I left the church and harmed or killed myself. This is the main point of this chapter. When someone clearly in distress is crying and you see this and still only ask if he is okay and he says *yes*, don't blindly accept that assertion without further inquiry. The difference between life and death can be a moment of more probing concern. In my view, the proper thing to do would be to say, *You do not look like you are okay. Why don't you stay here for a while and talk to me about what is bothering you* (or words to that effect)?

My point earlier was the need to start caring more for our fellow humans and that means taking the time to diagnose the problem. My mother-in-law is correct: the first hundred years are indeed the hardest, but they don't have to be fatal if we only turn our focus away from ourselves and toward those we know are in distress. It was no surprise that my life was ripped apart and that I had crawled into my shell. No real calculus had to be done to understand this. I will always wonder why it was such a great mystery.

People say a divorce is like a death and though that is somewhat true in the sense there is a loss, death is rarely accompanied by the destruction of the survivor's self-esteem. Apart from murder and negligent homicides, which is irrelevant here, people don't typically die because of someone else. Divorce, on the other hand, leaves one feeling all the stages of grief with a few additions: the feelings of being kicked to the curb, unwanted, unloved, and undesired.

Anyway, I left my contact information with the office staff and waited for the call from my parish priest. About a week later, that call came while I was visiting a client at the jail. The caller ID merely said the name of the Church. I quickly excused myself from assisting my client and took the call. To my dismay, it was not my priest but the parish nun.

My first thought was relief. I had someone with a direct line of communication with God on the phone with me. I said, *Sister, thank you so much for calling. I am trying to meet with Father.* Sister asked me a few questions about the topic, and I stated I was in a pivotal place in my life and needed his prayers. Having experienced firsthand the power of his prayers during our first meeting, I had every reason to believe relief resided in the palms of his healing hands.

Unfortunately, Sister told me that is not what Father does, which I took to mean pray over select individuals. She asked me if I went to the church, and I replied *yes*. She then asked whether Father knew me. I explained I had already met him once or twice and he prayed over me, after which I felt the weight of the world lifted from me. I needed that again. She reiterated that is not what Father does, which left me puzzled because I honestly thought that praying over those in need is precisely what a priest does. She suggested instead I seek counseling through Catholic Charities.

I had been to Catholic Charities before and found the name to be a bit of a misnomer. I found nothing Catholic or even Christian about their counseling. I felt determined to see the priest and although I was extremely polite, I was somewhat persistent about needing to see the priest—my priest. I was convinced that fifteen minutes with my priest would bring me out of my depression. Unfortunately, I was again told I needed to seek counseling at Catholic Charities.

I will never forget the nun reciting the number to Catholic Charities once to me over the phone and then hanging up on me. I was stunned and appalled at the same time. I came away not filled with the holy spirit but with nothing, nada, zilch.

I had been a member of the parish for 20-plus years and Sister had just hung up on me. It only goes to show that people who outwardly portray themselves as holy are not always what they appear. As disheartened and grief-stricken as I was, I returned to the attorney panel to finish with my client. For me, this was a new low and yet I knew between the Holy Bible app and my own capacity to speak directly to God, I would survive another day and at that point that is all I could hope for or count on.

CHAPTER 11
HOME ALONE TOO

I always heard it was possible to break a person's spirit by depriving him of sleep, food, and other life essentials. I grew up hearing horror stories about the so-called Hanoi Hilton, the prisoner of war facility in North Korea where captured American soldiers and airmen were held and tortured for years. And of course, we are all familiar with the concentration camps setup during the Nazi regime and genocidal atrocities that occurred during the holocaust.

I have also witnessed how many of my clients changed and not always for the better by spending a short period of time in confinement. I witnessed countless grown men cry as they made their way back to the holding cell after being given a lengthy prison sentence. Why the governing organization overseeing prisons is still called the Department of "Corrections" is beyond me. I obviously never served any jail or prison sentence, but my time in exile was foisted upon me during a time that Covid and quarantines still had all of us in its grips.

My children had come home to stay during the time most businesses were closed. They had to work at home and, therefore, could really work anywhere if they had an internet connection.

Though Covid delivered a devastating blow to the economy and to many who lost loved ones, a few advantages came along too, like being able to have food and groceries delivered contact free or curb-side and being able to work from anywhere. For the first time in many years, my wife and I were able to spend a significant amount of time with our children, an opportunity that sadly, regardless of Covid or any other virus, will never be repeated.

Soon after the more severe restrictions were abated, my son and daughter left our home and went back to New York and New Jersey. I think their departure was a contributing factor to my wife's and my untimely marital demise. My wife's entire family, including uncles, aunts, and cousins, lived in and around New York and New Jersey and now my children were living there too. As far as family was concerned, my wife and I were living alone in Virginia.

Neither my family nor hers were in proximity. Considering my wife and I had grown apart, it was not surprising she chose to leave. The calculus was simple: Stay alone with me in Virginia or leave and be near everyone with whom she loved and who loved her, including her children.

Right or wrong, I felt my wife's ties to her family were so strong and the magnetic pull of New York was so equally powerful that I could set our car on autopilot and make the trip. Conversely, for her family to visit us ostensibly required them to travel through the Van Allen radiation belts.

I was often frustrated and annoyed having to always make the trip from Virginia to New York and back. We would make this not-so-scenic trip along the New Jersey Turnpike, especially during the holidays. Nary a time went by when, as we were pulling away, we were asked when we would return. I so much wanted to say *you are welcome to come visit us anytime in Virginia*, but I knew that would only start an argument with my wife, which would make for an uncomfortable and seemingly longer car ride.

Try as I might, when it came to her family, my statements never came out right. I suppose I am not very good at suppressing my innermost feelings. I also knew I had to spend the next eight or nine hours in the car while her family members each got to relax, so I allowed my resentment to fester. Resentment isn't a healthy feeling in any relationship and I should have done more to quash it, but my job was stressful and I needed weekends to relax, not to get stuck in traffic. Dread often set in as I thought about the next day of work after making that long, tedious drive.

Anyway, shortly after my children returned to New York, my wife left. I was left alone for a brief period until I could convince her to return. I was on the proverbial rollercoaster of emotions for two or three brief separation periods, but I never thought she would eventually leave for good.

As she made her way back home, I was straightening up the bathroom when I stumbled across a collection of books on life after marriage. I never was one to check her phone or go through her things. This is such a massive invasion of privacy that I never even contemplated it. My discovery was purely accidental and yet fortuitous. I began by reading some of the dog-eared pages in several of her books, trying to understand what she was thinking.

Shortly after my discovery, I thought I would pull out all the stops. I had promised her just after we were married, I would take her to Asheville, North Carolina. That is all I knew at that time. During our marriage, we traveled to such places as France, Italy, England, Spain, Malta, and a multitude of other exotic places, but I had made a promise to her and wanted to fulfill it. I made all the reservations, planned our routes, and executed the plan with military precision.

During the first leg of our trip, we stayed at the Grove Park Inn, a famous resort hotel built on the face of a mountain. The magnificent Grove Park Inn has hosted countless celebrities and dignitaries since its opening in 1913. As we checked in, I told the receptionist about my promise and the last time I had been at the Grove Park Inn, when all I could afford was a glass of ice water on the picturesque terrace. The front desk receptionist was so moved she grabbed the attention of the manager who then upgraded us to one of the finest rooms in the Inn and later had a very exquisite and expensive bottle of French Champagne and chocolate-dipped strawberries delivered to our room along with a very sweet handwritten card.

Life seemed good at that very moment. But just as all good things must come to an end, this trip was no exception, and it was a mere three to four weeks before my wife was sucked back to New York by its magnetic forces. This time, her departure was permanent.

Although I have always had an outgoing and witty personality, for reasons I am only starting to understand, I do not have many close friends. I often heard my oldest brother say to have a friend, one must be a friend. This concept seemed facially simple, but it became my undoing. I realized during my period of solitude that I failed miserably at being a friend to others.

I could be the life of any party when I needed to be. I was gregarious, honest, trustworthy, and I had a good working knowledge of almost any topic one might care to discuss. One should suppose friends like me would be in high demand, but my friendships and social life were largely the construct of my ex-wife. When she left for good, so too did my circle of *friends*. I had only one or two friends. I had only one or two friends in my own right.

Having miserably failed the test, my brother enunciated about friendship, left me with perilously too few people to call. As importantly, it left me with a paltry number of people who would care enough to call me. Not one to impose on people, I felt uncomfortable reaching out to others for what I considered self-serving reasons. I had no one—literally no one. I was in my own version of the Hanoi Hilton and, with each passing day, I felt my spirit break. I slipped back into a depression that was quickly followed up with massive burning anxiety.

I think the most frustrating part for me was that no one—save one or two of my so-called friends—including my neighbors, ever reached out to me in an entire year. As of this writing, I have surpassed the three hundred-and sixty-five-day mark by a healthy margin, and they have yet to call just to see how I am or to see whether I am dead or alive.

One would think a neighbor whose home I visited often with my wife might have come over with a plate of pasta or something. Better yet, a simple invitation to hang out on any given night would have been incredibly welcomed. It says to me they either lived in a bubble unfazed by my plight or they just did not care. I tend to think it is the latter and I am now okay with their decision, but only because I am in a much healthier place.

I am still not ecstatic about their decisions, but I am a firm believer in karma. It is said karma will do what karma always does. Inevitably, they will find themselves in a bind and someone will treat them in-kind. Maybe this sounds cold and spiteful, but knowing people exist who have little to no regard for me has temporarily hardened my heart.

One day, I spoke to a dear friend I have known for several decades. She knew what I was going through and blamed my wife for everything. I tried to explain it was not all her fault. Again, our story is complicated and does not need to be discussed here, but rest assured, I accept not only my own faults but also my role in the dissolution of my marriage. My friend knew I was depressed and asked if I was going to do anything to harm myself. I told her I really didn't know. She asked if I had any guns in my house. I told her I had a Glock 9mm next to my bed. She asked me if she could store it for me.

I knew if I was going to kill myself, I would not use a gun. My idea of suicide involved taking just about every pill I had and drifting off to sleep until my heart stopped. Again, I really love *life*. I simply wanted the pain, depression, and burning anxiety to subside. Deep down, I thought a lot about active suicidal ideations, meaning I had the intent to commit suicide, but if I had been saved I would have been just fine with that too. Nevertheless, I agreed to give her my handgun, along with all the magazines.

Truth be told, I have a safe full of guns and rifles, but at that moment my brain was in such a state of fog I could not remember the code to enter my own safe. I truly appreciated her gesture, however. She did more than anyone else I know during my depression. She took an affirmative step to remove a weapon I could have been used to end my own life.

The most life-changing event for me (prior to Judyth moving in with me) was when, after a year's time, my middle brother, Mark, moved in. He had been through a divorce many years prior and has lived with his own heartaches that are horrific and more than book-worthy, but I will leave that to him. I will only say he was extremely generous to his ex-wife, and that left him with little more than the clothes on his back.

On the other hand, his ex-wife outwardly appears to be living in the lap of luxury, having gotten nearly all his money and inheriting a sizable portion of her father's estate. My brother has many times discussed moving to a third-world country because the cost of living is so low that he could live out the remainder of his life on one or two dollars a day. His most recently planned destination was Guyana. Ironically, hordes of people are moving north to the United States for a better life, while my brother thought of moving south to their country for the exact reason.

When Mark called me, his lease was about to expire, and he really had no viable plan of action. He actually flew to Guyana to look at options there, but realistically, that was an unworkable consideration. Unlike the United States, that seems to take every emigrant who can successfully navigate the southern border, third-world countries have stringent citizen restrictions. One cannot just waltz into any other country, set up residency, declare citizenship, and be rewarded financially for having done so.

My arrangement with Mark was setting itself up to be quite workable. He needed a place to live within the United States and I desperately needed human interaction with someone who was my own flesh and blood. I unhesitatingly offered up my house, and he accepted.

I literally counted the days until his arrival, but he dropped off a truck and trailer load of his belongings and then left for another week and a half or so. As New Yorkers would say, I broke his balls over that decision for many weeks that followed, but his permanent arrival signified the beginning of the new beginning for me. I was finally able to start my life over again.

In essence, I was finally released from the Hanoi Hilton. However, for the longest time, my mind continued to transport me back to those times when I was sitting in my car alone at night or in my house on a weekend my brother left to visit his family or his girlfriend. The loneliness and the feelings that no one cared about me came flooding right back, and they were almost unbearable.

CHAPTER 12
GOT APPS PERHAPS?

For the first time in 31 years, I was truly alone. My wife moved out in earnest and had resolved never to return. Sure, I had a Golden Retriever, but this time, the solitude of being without a life partner was a precursor to the most dreadful time of my life.

As I expressed in an earlier chapter, my wife and I had few friends but no family in the vicinity. My answer to my wife's audacious move from my life and our marriage was to go onto not one but four dating apps. I needed to validate I still had it, whatever *it* meant.

I was told by many women not to worry; I was a good catch. I often facetiously retorted that a 15 inch Striped Bass was also a good catch, but it was not legally a keeper and had to be thrown back into the water. Now I realize my feeble attempt at humor probably made me out to be a smart ass.

Interestingly, the very opportunity I had to date as many women as I wanted and to have unlimited sex was never at the forefront of my thoughts. I wanted to love and be loved for what I had on the inside, not for my sexual prowess I knew was well past its prime, anyway. I did not go on many dates, but one was rather funny in a strange sort of way.

About halfway through the date, the woman asked me if I had been vaccinated. Without explaining my reasoning, I said *no*. She literally moved away from me and we spent the rest of the evening keeping a healthy social distance of six feet. Dr. Anthony Fauci would have been proud, although candidly I didn't care then and don't care now what Fauci thinks. But I did believe the question and the woman's reaction were strange.

We never went out again, even though she texted me multiple times. Suffice it to say, we kept a significantly greater social distance after she exposed her irrational fear of Covid-19 within a 6-foot radius as if viruses are stationary. It has since been revealed that the 6-foot social distance was an arbitrary number not backed by science at all.

I had always heard about dating apps, but never thought I would need to use one. Just after my wife left for New York, my self-esteem had become tattered and I was looking for some sign—any sign—I was still desirable. I got a dopamine rush each time a woman viewed my profiles and even more of a rush if she liked me and cared to text me.

Shopping for relationships on dating apps is interesting, to say the least. The entire process is superficial because it is almost based entirely on looks. It was easy to take a two second look at someone and decide then and there whether she was the right match. If she had the slightest imperfection, it was a simple swipe to the left on my smartphone. If she had potential, it was a swipe to the right.

If I ever thought a woman was attractive, only then I read her profile. Disappointment often set in as some of the women I found attractive had written in their profiles such things as *if you voted for Trump keep swiping* or *if you're not vaccinated keep swiping*. I was left to wonder whether these women sincerely wanted to meet someone.

Profiles were sometimes provocative and somewhat shocking too, like those in which women were seeking a third person to join her and her mate in bed. I wanted nothing to do with any of that mess and was really searching for love.

Online dating was frustrating and filled with scammers. I am certain women's pictures are stolen and fake profiles are set up just to entice men into giving out enough information about themselves to consummate the scam. I was the victim of just such a scam.

I was not dumb enough to give out my social security number or other identifying information, but once a person gives a scammer his full name and cellphone number, it is easy for anyone with even minimal skills to find just about anything either on the dark web or by doing a reverse phone number lookup. Getting hacked anytime is never easy or pleasant, but getting hacked in the middle of an emotional crisis must be worse.

When I was hacked, the culprits commandeered my work email account and started sending emails disguised as me to everyone I knew. Several people called and asked if I had sent them an email. Thankfully, the email looked suspicious enough

before they opened the viral and malicious attach-
ment it contained.

My Facebook account was completely stolen and
because the scammers had somehow redirected
my email account, I was unable to reset the password to regain control. I suspect a decade's worth
of my photographic life is being used to set up fake
profiles in faraway places. I still have no personal
Facebook and do not intend on creating a new one.

At the same time my email and Facebook were
being hacked, I received a call from Blockfi, a cryptocurrency exchange, where I kept Bitcoin and
Ethereum. At first, I thought the call itself was a
scam, but after calling the number back, I realized
it was legitimate.

The caller was from Blockfi cybersecurity, and he
told me someone tried to withdraw my Bitcoin from
my account. I didn't have a sizable stake in Bitcoin,
but it was still worth tens of thousands of dollars—
money I obviously did not care to lose, especially
given the self-induced financial crisis in which I
found myself. I was able to save my Bitcoin and
Ethereum, but was not so lucky with a few other
coins and tokens. I was scammed out of roughly
$8,000.00 and there was nothing I could do about it.

The scammers had coopted my office from a place of law to a makeshift command center as we went to general quarters, trying to beat them to their next scam. My office tempo reminded me of my days working at the National Response Center after the Exxon Valdez oil tanker had run aground and was discharging crude oil, except that I had to play every role in the Incident Command System. My secretary and I chaotically and frantically tried to notify everyone who could safeguard my assets, but the scammers seemed to always be one or two steps ahead of us.

I remember barking out orders to my secretary to change passwords as quickly as she could. At that moment, I did not care what the password was as long as I knew what it was not. My secretary gave me the new password; it began with D.o.a.b.h, an acronym that stood for *die of a broken heart*. I was not expecting that, but I suppose I couldn't complain.

We also froze credit card accounts and locked down every digital and electronic asset I had. The scammers are professionals and know far more about computers and digital footprints than I will ever know, so to attempt to outwit them seemed an impossible task.

At every turn, it appeared someone was gunning for me. As they say on the radio, the hits just kept on coming until I finally got exasperated with on-line dating. I found women online largely fell into the following categories: those who wanted to *jump my bones* at the first opportunity and told me those exact words; those who were opportunists and only saw me for what they thought I could provide; and those who were *catfish*, a term that refers to people who put pictures on their profiles that are either completely fictitious or grossly out of date. After I got catfished a few times, I decided to significantly scale back online dating.

The fourth category is scammers. These are the bottom dwellers of the online dating world. They are probably not women at all, but men who set up fake accounts. These scavengers use stolen pictures for the sole purpose of gathering as much intelligence information as possible for hacking into bank accounts, cryptocurrency accounts, email accounts, Facebook accounts, etc. These people are despicable because they prey on the vulnerabilities of people who, for a variety of reasons, are searching for love and companionship.

After a period, I began to see common characteristics to help me identify scammers. They usually had between one to four photos on their profiles. Anytime they engaged in conversation, the first or second sentence was nearly always, how long have you been on the app and what are looking for on here—literally those exact words.

The next most common characteristic was the *women* usually lived somewhere within proximity but always tended to be traveling abroad, usually in Europe. Alternatively, they were originally from Europe but had only been in the United States for a short time. These scammers aren't stupid. They realize men are suckers for a sexy European accent.

Finally, and this was the most obvious indication of a scammer, whenever you wanted to take it to the next level by doing a video chat or simply wanted to verify they were who they said they were, their phones never worked. Their phones worked fine for texting, but never for chatting. Scammers also say they never check dating apps and want you to go to WhatsApp or their snapchat account.

One of the strangest nights of my life bar none, was the night I began chatting with a woman I met on an app who sent me nude pictures of herself and then proceeded to tell me what she wanted to sexually do with me. Anyway, I met this woman at a restaurant, and we had a nice dinner. Afterward, she agreed to follow me home, where it was all but agreed we would have some form of intimacy. I left the restaurant with her following close behind.

At some point, I checked my rearview mirror and realized she was gone. I pulled over at the earliest opportunity and texted her to see if she had gotten lost. I waited and waited until suddenly a text appeared that said *I am sorry. You are a nice guy. I can't do this to you.*

I have no idea what that meant, but I have the distinct feeling she was either planning to rob me, accuse me of rape, or extort money from me. I really have no idea. Sometimes it pays to be a nice guy. In the year following my separation, I probably received more unsolicited nudes than Hugh Hefner. But again, I was not looking for sex, I was looking for love.

I reserved what I consider to be the fifth and most precious category of women because these legitimate women hold a special place in my heart. Those are the women with whom I had shared experiences and with whom I could always count on for candid, honest conversation. These were usually not women I dated, but women who genuinely seemed to care about me as much as I cared about them. I cherish these women to this day and believe I always will.

The frustrations with online dating left me home alone most of the time, making me vulnerable to the whims of my mind, and my mind did not always fairly treat me. It would concoct situations that were not necessarily reality based but which at the time seemed all too real.

Loneliness is a mind killer. We are human beings. We are social beings who crave interaction and, to a lesser extent, approval and acceptance from other human beings. I feel confident stripping a person of this fundamental need is the main reason prisoners are put in solitary confinement. The quiet desolation one feels when persistently alone is maddening.

I once heard about a cuddling service. From what I understand, this is not a front for sex, but rather a bona fide business where a man pays a woman to spend time cuddling with him. When I first read about it prior to my separation, I thought it was the dumbest thing I had ever heard about. I wondered who came up with that cockamamie idea and even more who would ever pay to be cuddled. But loneliness is brutal and spares no one.

I do not have the medical data to support this assertion, but it has always been common knowledge that people who spend their time alone die much sooner than those who do not. If that is true, and I have every reason to think it is, I understand. As animals, we not only desire interaction and touch, but we also crave it. Touch is a central part of wholistic wellness from both a mental and physical health perspective.

CHAPTER 13

MY DEADBEAT TENANT AND HIS MERRY BAND OF GOONS

What you are about to read, I believe, is the single most detrimental thing that caused me to finally snap during my entire year-long ordeal. I previously discussed the Cedar Road rental property and how I was intending to use it for my new legal office. I had rented the house for about seven years and had greatly profited. Those tenants had notified me that they were moving out to purchase their own home.

I wanted to rent the house again but also now had an opportunity to make additional repairs and upgrades and to rent the house for more money. I never raised the rent on my initial tenants, thinking if I had tenants who paid on time and respected the home, I would reward them with a rent freeze. The additional rent would not have altered my life in any meaningful way, but I figured any increase could have been significant enough for my tenants to look for another place. I was unwilling to take that gamble.

The house was essentially operating on autopilot and was one fewer thing I needed to worry about. Besides, the initial renters took a chance on this house when it sat vacant and neglected for years prior to my purchase.

Consequently, over the course of their tenancy, they discovered multiple things about the house that needed to be repaired and they were always kind about it when they could have exhibited renter's remorse or asked for a reduction in rent. I think the reason these things never happened was because I was Johnny-on-the-spot when it came to repairing anything that needed repairing. I was the direct opposite of the bumlord I had when I lived in the trailer.

A long-time former client, a guy I considered a friend, had expressed an interest in renting from me. This was a guy who had spent a significant time in prison but who was fundamentally a decent chap, at least when it came to me, maybe because I was his attorney and had gone above and beyond to keep him out of prison for long durations.

Several times, he had also come to my rescue when I needed something done to that very house or to the marital property. He was a go-to guy for anything I needed. If he could not fix what needed to be fixed, he knew another guy who could. He grew up painting. His father was a master painter and Don had also mastered the trade. I have never seen anyone paint quite like him. He was incredible.

Renting the house to Don was a win-win situation, I thought. I would keep the rent below fair market value and he would, in turn, make the additional repairs and upgrades to the house. I always knew Don had a propensity for skidding off the rails, but this time he seemed mentally and fiscally stable.

He had a good job with a reliable company. I know because I did the employment check. Our relationship was shaping up to be mutually beneficial. Unfortunately, I did not listen to my gut brain that was telling me not to rent to him. Consequently, our newly formed business relationship turned into a nightmare.

Don and I first got acquainted when I was court-appointed to his case in 2004. I recall once when my wife and I were having dinner, he called me about a problem he had with the jail. He was supposed to serve time on weekends and the jail said he was late and needed to do his time in straight confinement. I immediately excused myself from dinner and drove to jail. I was able to smooth things over with the deputies at the jail and kept Don on the weekend program. Our friendship was forged at that moment.

Don reciprocated when my builder, who was constructing a room addition for my home, walked off the job. Don asked how much was left on the contract and then agreed to complete the job for that amount. Afterward, I hired Don for small jobs, here and there, and he hired me as needed.

Around 2014, Don had gotten charged with his third DUI offense, along with a violation of probation. This time, there was little I could do. He was sentenced to serve seven years or so with the Virginia Department of Corrections.

Twice I met him at Sussex II Virginia State Penitentiary to discuss a Workers Compensation claim I was handling for him. I recall the ominous site of the Penitentiary and only imagined what it was like to be housed there. I remember taking pictures of the guard towers and the prison fencing complete with barbed wire and razor-sharp concertina wire.

Before venturing inside to visit with Don, I stood in silence and took a mental picture of the facility. It was an eerie sight. Once inside, I was practically stripped searched before being allowed to enter the main facility. It mattered not that I was an attorney. From the prison's perspective, anyone, regardless of position or status, was capable of snuggling weapons and narcotics into the facility. They did not take any chances.

After a short time, Don was wheeled into the conference-style waiting area where I was seated. He seemed relieved to see a friendly face, and I did not think too much about his wheelchair because I knew Don had injured himself when he fell off a ladder while painting, hence the workers' compensation claim.

As it turned out, Don never really needed a wheelchair. He had simply outsmarted the system. He knew his handicap improved his chances of survival in prison. After all, who wants to fight a man in a wheelchair? He also knew he would be given special dispensations as a handicapped person.

The only trouble was the entire handicap was a charade—a farce. He paid some poor sap fifty cents a day to be wheeled around everywhere he needed to go.

Don loved to tell the story about the day of his release from prison. His guards wheeled him out to the main courtyard, and they told him he was free to leave. The guard then asked him what he wanted to do about the wheelchair. Without uttering a word, Don stood up and walked away, telling the guard he would not need the chair. According to Don, the guard's jaw dropped, and he said something along the lines of *praise Jesus, he has been healed.*

Don is a master manipulator. He could talk his way in or out of just about anything. His friends used to say Don was such a good bullshitter, he could sell an ice cube to an Eskimo. I knew Don was gifted in many ways, and I was keenly aware of his ability to scam the system—any system, or any person, for that matter.

Months before he went to prison, he tried to entice my wife and me to invest in some houses he was flipping. He invited us over to his house and grilled a pile of choice cut steak and all the fixings. He then hit us with the hard sell. Everything sounded too good to be true and we are all patently aware of the corollary to *if it sounds too good to be true.*

Thankfully, my wife was insistent about not investing any of our money. Don went belly up and lost hundreds of thousands of investor's dollars but none of ours. I credit my wife with making the decision to abstain from that investment, and I credit myself for listening to her for a change.

When Don asked about renting my full-time rental home, I was of course well-versed with all his get-rich-quick schemes and his inability to state the simple truth and yet despite the aforementioned investment scheme, I felt, as his lawyer, I was immune to his chicaneries. Certainly, he would not treat his lawyer the way he treated everyone else. I had done so much for him over the years, and I was a lawyer, after all. I felt sure he would not try his manipulative antics on me.

I may not have been streetwise, but I was well-versed in the law. Don knew that first-hand. Besides, Don was still my go-to guy and would step up at a moment's notice to help fix anything that went wrong with any property I owned. Often, he fixed things for nothing more than beer money. I felt if there was one person in the world who was safe from his manipulative ways, it was I. Unfortunately, my wife was not around to talk some sense into me. She had already established her new residence in New York.

When the time came to re-rent my house, Don laid it on thick and I bit hook, line, and sinker. He promised to repair and re-stain the wooden deck, paint the house, sand and refinish the hardwood floors and tile areas of the kitchen, among other things. The allure of this free labor was too good to pass up. In exchange for his services, I told him I would rent the home to him for hundreds of dollars less than fair market value.

I regretted my decision to rent to Don from day one. I do not know who Don's enemies were, but they never missed a chance to sabotage the house. They clogged plumbing pipes, ripped down insulation in the crawl space, disconnected duct work for the HVAC system and bent the coils in the window air-conditioning units so the units would not sufficiently draw outside air to cool. I was left holding the bag, as I could not say who was doing what.

Anytime rent was due, Don came up with multiple excuses for why rent would be late. These ranged from he just got a new job and his pay was withheld to the bank screwed up his deposit or someone must have stolen the cashier's check out of my mailbox where he claimed to place it.

I was left every month to stress about whether I would get paid the rent he owned me. Finally, he just stopped paying. He lived in my house for two solid months, rent free, but not only him. He invited his band of goons to live with him. These included his cousin, a prescription drug abuser, an elderly woman, and a crack cocaine addict.

Don later complained I was not entitled to receive rent because I did not evict the very people he invited to live with him. The whole cast of characters living in that home was something out of *Ripley's Believe it or Not,* or PT Barnum's freak show. His cousin was so drugged up he would lie around all day making animal noises. Physically, he appeared human, but his behavior was the strangest I have ever encountered in my life. If I had closed my eyes, I could have envisioned a sort of Therianthrope—someone who is human for part of the time and animal for the other part.

The elderly woman they nicknamed *mom* was a rather sweet woman, apparently tasked with kitchen duties. Every time I went over to the house attempting to collect rent, I observed *mom* minding the stove and stirring the pot. My nose was instantly filled with the putrid pungency of Hamburger Helper. That seemed to be their cuisine of choice. The crack cocaine addict was there only briefly because she violated her probation for the fourth time for, of all things, failing a drug screen, and was sentenced to serve an active prison sentence.

I detected a chink in Don's tough, prison-hardened armor within weeks after renting to him. He was starting to lose his mind. He lost his job and tried to cover it up. His claim was he was only moving up to a better job with more money and perks. That cycle continued week in and week out until the story got a little too repetitive for my liking.

The excuses for his inability or unwillingness to pay rent were ubiquitous. I was aware of Don's criminal history, but I never viewed him as a reprobate. But I had to accept that I had been snookered, and I had to find a way to get Don and his merry band of goons out of my house.

I truly believe this situation had more to do with my meltdown than any other. This was the proverbial straw that broke the camel's back. I simply could not believe the audacity of Don and his goons to live in the very home I paid for with my labor, and then almost dare me to do anything about it. Once when I drove by the house and saw cars in the driveway, I totally lost my shit. I made a U-turn and pulled in and pounded on the door. I told them they all needed to go. I am not aware of a time when I was angrier than at that very moment.

Don reacted by yelling back at me and then inviting me to go outside to fight. He assumed a pugilistic stance and began shadowboxing the way Mohammed Ali did during his warmups. The only concerning thing for me was Don's threat to kill me. I knew Don was truculent and cared so little for human life that unless I got the upper hand in our skirmish, he would carry out his threat.

I knew at that moment I had to either think about my Krav Maga and jiu jitsu training and be prepared to fight or de-escalate the situation. One of the precepts engrained in all students of martial arts is that walking away is always preferable to fighting. I told Don I would defend myself, but he needed to understand he was on probation; I was not. If he attempted to strike me, he would be going back to prison. I would be in the clear. Don backed off, and we eventually had a civil conversation in the driveway.

I tried my hardest to be cordial to Don, but his mind seemed to have deteriorated to the point of no return. He was absolutely convinced someone was hacking into his phone and was trying to frame him for some inconspicuous crime that would send him back to prison. Nearly every day, Don had a new phone with a new number and then he would call me to tell me how, only moments after getting the phone, it had been hacked. He said Verizon told him the hacker had CIA level skills. I am convinced there were never any hackers, and Verizon told him that to appease him.

As hard as I tried to get Don to accept simple logic, his paranoia grew stronger with each passing day. I know of the expression just because you're paranoid doesn't mean they're not out to get you. But nothing Don said made any sense. As much as I tried to talk about my rent and the sabotage of my house, he redirected the conversation to his cellular phones and the perceived hacking. Looking back, I was being gaslighted by Don and it was working. As hard as I tried to get off the topic of his phones, the angrier he became with me for failing to believe his story.

I finally got fed up with Don and called in reinforcement in the form of a client who had spent a decade in prison and who would do anything to back me up. I tried as much as possible not to do anything resembling illegal behavior, but the temptation was overwhelming.

Several times I called my former client, who I will only identify as '*A*,' to handle the situation, only to back out. *A* was raring to go. This was the sort of thing he lived for, but I was trying my best not to end up in prison for having thrown Don and his goons out on their heads or to make them disappear as A had suggested.

I had to drive by the rental house every day because it was on the way to court. Every time I passed it, the wound opened wider. If Don had fallen on hard times and asked me if he could stay in my house, I may have said *yes*, but this felt completely different. I was being given the biggest *fuck you* I ever received in my life. I believe most people would say I am a kind and generous person who would give not only the shirt but every garment I own to just about anyone who politely asked. But I have little regard for swindlers and thieves.

I never saw my materialistic things as bragging points. They were purchased for specific reasons or acquired with the intention of sharing them with those I love. Don never allowed me to give him the shirt off my back. He ripped it off me and dared me to take it back.

I had represented many people on both sides of the *v*, as we say in civil law parlance. In other words, I had represented both landlords (plaintiffs) trying to evict, and I had represented tenants (defendants) trying to stay as long as they possibly could.

Until now, I always thought of landlord/tenant law as a game of cat and mouse. If I represented the landlord, obviously I wanted to get an order of possession of the residence as soon as possible. If I represented a tenant, I wanted to do everything I could within the letter of the law to delay any court action that would result in eviction.

One surefire way to delay a civil court action is to make an initial appearance and then ask a judge to order a Bill of Particulars. This is essentially asking the court to require the plaintiffs to put in writing their justification for eviction. This simple request can delay a case for two months, allowing tenants to reside rent free during that period. I never really understood the psychological effects this request has on landlords who are people just like me and not big corporations who are not personally invested.

If I could make one request to the General Assembly of Virginia, it would be to change the rules in landlord and tenant cases. Having gone through the process, and understanding the brutal mind fuck that takes place, it is my recommendation that the clerk of the civil court immediately send out a form for tenants to complete at the time of an unlawful detainer (i.e., eviction) filing. The goal should be to settle these cases as soon as possible to avoid the psychological harm done to those getting screwed over—typically landlords.

I eventually filed an unlawful detainer naming myself as the plaintiff and had to wait for an extra thirty days just for the initial hearing in which my tenants could then ask for a Bill of Particulars. I also had gotten word my tenants were planning to call in sick on the initial appearance to delay even the initial appearance. All one had to say was the word Covid and a continuance of the case was assured. That was their plan.

I knew there was only one thing I could do. Having been Don's lawyer for many years taught me one valuable thing—Don responded better with kindness than with threats. I cozied up to Don and tried my best to reason with him. I thought if I could convince him to leave on his own accord, I could get him out much sooner.

The real estate market was already softening, and interest rates were on the rise. I knew if I did not get him out of that house soon, my chances of selling that house would greatly reduce and I was certain not to get the benefit of a bidding war that was so common during a time when demand for houses outnumbered supply.

I also knew the school year was fast approaching and any prospective buyer would want to be settled into a home prior to that date. I feverishly, but calmly, began texting Don. I finally convinced him to leave after sending him a letter stating I would not seek any back rent or any of my court costs. That seemed like a small price to pay to get him out of my house.

Don finally texted me back from one of his many phones and said he would agree to move, but only needed a little more time. His projected move-out date was roughly one week before we were due to go to court for the initial appearance. I felt relief for the first time in a long time, although I knew nothing Don said could ever be taken as gospel. Again, Don was a master manipulator. If his lips were moving, he was probably lying. I resisted the temptation to engage him further. I merely said, *Thank you* and let it be.

About a week prior to his expected departure, I went to the house and saw nothing was being done in contemplation of his move out. Mom was cooking her usual Hamburger Helper and Don's cousin was lying on the couch making animalistic sounds and mumbling incoherently to himself.

It was like going into a house of horrors. The entire experience seemed surreal. Not a single packed box was visible, and items in the home remained undisturbed. I politely, but rhetorically, asked how the move was going. I was told it was going well, though obviously it had not even begun. I left feeling once again I have been shafted.

The significant part of this story is it was all happening at the same time my business (and thus my income) had dried up. I was having to pay my wife spousal support, and I was still reeling from intense depression, anxiety, and lack of self-esteem. I was responsible for paying my primary mortgage, the mortgage on the house on Cedar Road, all the office expenses, a boat payment, marina storage fees, a car payment, and most important, spousal support at a time when I was being shafted at every turn.

Had Don simply paid his rent, one of those pressures could have been abated. To top it off, I had an impending jury trial and was in no mental shape to handle it. I did not know what to do.

I later texted Don about what I had seen and was told he had checked every U-Haul place in the vicinity and was unable to locate one. He also told me even if he could get one, he was not sure he could afford it because his cousin was not helping with rent.

At this point, I had a real estate agent because I knew at some point the goon squad would be gone and I wanted to sell the home. I just did not know when that time would arise. I told her about the U-Hauls, and she quickly did a search of her own and found there were U-Hauls aplenty.

I texted Don that not only a U-Haul truck had been located but that he would not have to pay for it. The cost was insignificant relative to the peace-of-mind his move-out would bring to me. Besides, I was facing Hobson's choice—either let Don continue to live in the house on his terms or pay to get him out.

On the day of the supposed move, I rented a 20-foot U-Haul truck and backed it up into the driveway of the house. I had rented the truck for a 24-hour period, and I felt relieved that finally my life was about to be normalized. I spent most of my time in the gym waiting to get periodic reports from my realtor, who told me she would keep the embers hot under Don to ensure the move happened as we had hoped.

We were up against the clock on the U-Haul rental. Our drop-dead time was 4:30 p.m. At that precise time, I needed to depart the house, drive to the storage unit, help off-load Don's furniture, and get the U-Haul back in time to check it in.

When my realtor called and said very few items were on the truck, again I snapped. I drove over to the house, enraged. Once again, I felt betrayed by Don. I had been manipulated into throwing good money after bad.

Good money? Hell, I was about to throw borrowed money after bad. As I got into my car, I decided I could not handle the matter alone. *A* had been chomping at the bit to help me throw the bums out and I had resisted his offer, but it was now go-time. I reached *A,* and he said he would meet me at the house.

I arrived first and went inside and literally lost my shit. Don was not even there, and his Therianthropic cousin was lying on his bed in the back bedroom. I wanted to beat his ass into oblivion, but I knew I would fare worse for having done so as I would surely be arrested for the assault and battery or worse.

I honestly don't know what would have happened had I begun to beat him. I had so much pent-up anger; I know not if or when I would have stopped beating him. Instead, I did a lot of yelling at him and even at mom but did nothing physical and ultimately went outside wondering what I could or should do next.

About that time, my friend *A* and his wife showed up. The cavalry had come just in the nick of time. My emotions finally boiled over and instead of acting out physically, I began to cry. Something had to give in my life. I just couldn't take it anymore.

A put his arm around my shoulder and we walked a short while until I could get my emotions under control. He told me he would be right back, and he went into the house to confront Don's Therianthropic cousin.

As soon as Don's cousin saw *A,* a shirtless black man who stood about six feet two inches tall and who has visible knife scars and gunshot entrance wounds, Don's cousin recoiled into the corner of his bed. I am one hundred percent certain he did not expect this man to appear. I later went in and both of us stood over Don's cousin, telling him in no uncertain terms it was time to leave.

For the rest of my life, I will never forget him yelling back at me as if I was in the wrong and the words that stung the most were *Whatever bud.* Those two words spoke volumes. The first told me he truly did not care that he was living in my house rent free as if he had a right to be there. The second said he did not have a modicum of respect for me to call me by my actual name. I left the house and walked over to the U-Haul.

The next thing I remember was punching the metal ramp leading to the U-Haul's near-empty truck bed with all my might. This action left my hand swollen for days, but at the time I felt no pain. Looking back, I am still quite surprised I didn't break my hand.

I do not think I consciously thought of the ramp as a proxy for any one individual. It was simply a target of opportunity for me to release the massive amount of adrenaline coursing through my body. At this very moment, the confluence of Don, the stresses of my job, triggers, the irrational fear of going broke, and the economic meltdown built to an unhealthy crescendo. The only thing I could think of to escape it all was taking my life.

My realtor, my friend *A*, and I began moving the few items out of the truck and into the garage. I had no choice but to empty the truck and drive it back for check in. Just as we were in the process of removing items from the truck, Don showed up. I suppose as stupid as it was, punching the ramp released my tension and helped me to calm down, because I was able to speak sensibly to Don. We quickly formulated a game plan with all four of us moving items.

We loaded that truck in record time, drove it to the storage unit, off-loaded it, and I got the U-Haul back to the rental company with not a minute to spare. I believe God saw me that day and recognized I needed an intervention. I thank God we got Don out of that house and without having to resort to violence.

As for Don's cousin, *A* told him he had better be out by 2:00 p.m. the following day or else. As I left court the next day and drove past the house about 11:00 a.m., I saw Don's cousin with a flatbed full of his items. He made a wise choice and finally came out of my house for good.

Neither Don nor his cousin knew *A* is a leader of the Bloods' street gang and has an entire cadre of Bloods ready to do whatever is necessary to support and defend me. I helped *A* in a criminal case, and his loyalty has been unwavering ever since. I did not want to go to prison myself for enlisting the help of the Bloods, but I was at my wit's end.

I am grateful that the situation among *A*, the remaining Bloods, Don, his goons, and I never got physical, but this taught me another lesson in just how far a person can be pushed into taking matters into his own hands. If nothing else, I am now able to identify with my criminal clients who sometimes choose not to exercise the same level of restraint and find themselves criminally charged.

Don was still holding on for another month along with mom. Every day he texted me with some reason why he could not move out. I was given one excuse after the next and he texted as though somehow he was doing me a favor by moving out.

Eventually I goaded him into accepting we were planning to change the locks and, the very next day, my realtor did just that. After the locks were changed, Don had the audacity to text me, proclaiming what my realtor did was illegal, as if his entitlement was superior to mine. In response, I took a screenshot of his text message in which he had agreed to the lock change, and he never texted me more about that topic. I have observed brazen behavior before, but this won the gold medal.

As for *A*, he still texts me regularly with words of encouragement and a reminder that he and his posse of Bloods are, and always will be, at my beck and call should I ever need them. I never knew until months later that *A* and five of his Bloods members went to the house to ensure it was clear. *A* later told me if it had not, the remaining tenants would have disappeared. I can only thank God Don and his goons had the good sense to leave when they did.

A is a faithful man who is turning his life around. He is still a leader of the Bloods, but his heart is in the right place. He did not have to show the restraint he showed during the Don debacle, but he did. He did not have to tell me he would do anything for me, a non-Bloods member, but he did. *A single handedly took charge of the situation and, as loyal as he is to me, I will continue to be just as loyal to him.*

CHAPTER 14
FATHER KNOWS BEST

The weekend of August 12, 2022 to August 14, 2022 was another major turning point in my life. This was the weekend of the Drum Corps International (DCI) finals event in Indianapolis, Indiana. My son had performed with one of the Corps—Troopers—for three summers in a row and the Troopers were expected to make finals again for the first time since he performed with them.

I loved drum corps even before he performed, but nothing quite beats seeing one's own son perform at a world class level at world class stadiums and arenas around the country. I was a percussionist with above-average skills, but he took percussion to a whole new level, one I could not have attained even at the peak of my ability. I could not have been prouder of his accomplishments. Drum corps, whose motto is Marching Music's Major League, is music, theater, athletics, precision, and costume design all rolled into one. For those who have no idea what I am talking about, I suggest you visit DCI.org.

When my son called me about my flying to Indy, I had massive trepidation. I had always been thrilled by the spectacle of drum corps and knew in my heart of hearts I would enjoy it. However, I was extremely worried about the triggering effect Indy and, more specifically, Lucas Oil Stadium and drum corps, would have on me because I would be going back to a place last visited with my wife. I thought about how I would feel.

Would I feel anxious? Would this be another wedding of sorts that would send my mind into a frenzy? I ignored my son's invitation, hoping he would forget about it as well. I also secretly hoped that Troopers would have a zero probability of making finals, which would ostensibly cause my son to be less interested in going.

When it appeared inevitable that Troopers would make finals, my son became more insistent. I was forced to decide, and I made my decision in favor of going. I needed to step outside my bubble—my safe zone—to test my mettle. Would I crash again, or would I survive? This is the question I needed to resolve for myself.

He very much wanted to go and did not want to go alone. I left all the details (e.g., hotel arrangements, tickets) up to him and that relieved my stress. All I had to do was to book my flight, and that was enough for me. I only needed to take a deep breath and brace for what I imagined would make me feel uncomfortable, if not worse. This is the question I needed to answer for myself. These sorts of internal battles all sound a little crazy and perhaps like much ado about nothing, but trust me, triggers are real and can cause extreme harm. Just ask a veteran suffering with post-traumatic stress disorder what the sound of fireworks does to his psyche.

My arrival at the airport was stress free. The line at the American Airlines ticket counter was longer than I can ever remember. A hundred people or more were lined up to check bags. I was worried I would miss my flight, but I handled it well.

Thankfully, a woman at the ticket counter recognized that many in the line would miss their flights and began asking those on specific flights to step out of line and to follow her. This left gaps in the remaining line. I moved up a little and passed a woman who had four or five bags and could not move them all forward at the same time.

I fully recognized she was ahead of me, and I was only moving up to close the gap. Engrossed in my own world with headphones on, I was listening to relaxing music when, suddenly, the woman started yelling at me for *cutting her off*. Despite my noise canceling headphones and music, her furious voice penetrated.

She was pissed off. I calmly removed my headphones and asked her what her problem was. She said I was being rude for cutting her off. I said I was only moving up, and I clearly acknowledged she was ahead of me. She kept going at it until finally I told her to chill out and to take a Valium. If only she knew what I was taking, she would have been shocked.

I previously spoke about karma, and how karma does what karma is going to do. Well, karma struck this woman when the American Airlines ticket agent called my flight, and I moved out of line again to follow her. I was heading up the escalator and looked back to see that the angry woman was still roughly in the same spot. I so wanted to say *have a nice flight* but resisted being an asshole, although it was awfully tempting.

Everything went much better than expected in Indy. I was not my usual happy-go-lucky self, but I was far better than I ever expected to be. I had braced for the worst, but the worst never happened. Although the triggers I worried about occurred, their effects were momentary.

I spent a lot more time resting in the hotel room than I ever would have in the past, but that is okay. My son seemed to recognize I needed some time to rest and relax. He never pressured me to go beyond my limits. The main thing was we were in Indy spending quality time with each other, and that was all that mattered to either of us.

I thoroughly enjoyed watching the drum corps as I had done in the past. I was living in the present moment and savoring all the musical flavors the corps had so richly prepared. Although I intermittently entertained thoughts of my wife and even my mother, both of whom had been there with me 13 years prior, neither of those thoughts consumed my mind as I feared they might.

My mother passed away from cancer in 2020. I was close to my mother, but I have certain regrets. Unfortunately, because my father and my relationship was often strained for reasons I still do not understand, my mother suffered. I failed to visit as often as I should have, even knowing she was terribly sick. However, I am happy I made the choice to visit with her a week before her passing.

Generally, the only way I could really spend mother/son time with her was by planning a trip for the two of us. She enjoyed drum corps as much as I did and going back to Lucas Oil Stadium for the first time since her passing and the separation from my wife, who also spent three summers going to Indy, was very much on my mind.

Yet, when DCI finals were over, I felt I had jumped over another massive hurdle. I was learning to do things alone for the first time in nearly 32 years. My son's persistence paid off for me and I will always be grateful that he never gave up on me when I was ready to give up on myself.

There was one rather funny thing that happened the first night I arrived. My son kept telling me he smelled something foul, like body odor. I knew it could not be me. I had showered, used deodorant, and applied cologne. But I had traveled and spent an afternoon in the sun watching the corps warm up. Was it me who stunk? I kept thinking it could not be because I was always attentive to my personal hygiene.

Nevertheless, I wondered if my anxiety was emitting an odor I could not smell. Once back at the hotel, he again said he thought it was me as I was passing him in my underwear in preparation for sleep. I said there was only one way to solve this problem—take a shower. But he had me wondering whether my body was giving off olfactory clues to my anxiety.

After I showered and was lying in bed, I made the decision to do a Boolean search on Google for anxiety and odors. If you ever made the mistake of searching for certain medical symptoms, then you know the search will often come back with something along the lines of *YOU ARE DYING. SEEK IMMEDIATE MEDICAL ATTENTION*. It can be an unwary trap for any person battling a generalized anxiety disorder.

Not surprisingly, the articles I read said that anxiety can release a certain hormone that may be undetectable by the person emitting it. Now I started to worry. Maybe I did smell bad and did not know it. I decided to text several women who knew me very well and who I believed would tell me the truth about any malodorous condition I might have. One text message exchange with a woman I will only identify as K went exactly like this:

Fri, Aug 12, 10:38 p.m.

Me: K are you awake?

K: I am

Me: If I ask you a question will you promise to give me an honest answer?

K: Yes sir

Me: You promise?

K: When have I never not given u an honest answer....

Me: Okay

I need to know this...

Do I smell of body odor? I know anxiety can cause people to smell. I need to know.

Be honest so I can fix the problem

K: OMG .... Rob .... Trust me when I tell u there is no

human that I come in contact with that smells better than u....

There is absolutely no problem

Me: Okay, my son told me I smelled but I didn't smell it. Then I googled it and I found out anxiety causes a horrible odor that a person may not notice

I mean I didn't smell it

I don't think I smell it but that's the point. Some people smell and don't realize it.

The text exchange went for a little longer, but you get the point. I was relieved to find out not only did I not stink, but I was flattered to find out that, at least according to K, I was one of the best smelling humans. If truth be told, I was relieved, but not completely surprised. I take no credit, however. Credit must go to the fragrance chemists at Versace.

Apart from the mystery stench, the weekend was fantastic. I enjoyed hanging out with my son and watching the incredible drum corps. This trip proved to me I could get my life back on track if only I set aside my fears. We are planning to return as often as we can regardless of whether the Troopers make finals.

Not to be outdone, my daughter arrived on September 30, 2022, because she had two weddings to attend. One wedding was in Maryland and she attended that one alone. The other was in Charlottesville, Virginia. She was allowed to bring a guest, and she invited me.

I was petrified to attend the wedding or to even go back to Charlottesville, a place that held so many great memories of my son at the University of Virginia, and yet I had committed to going. I was so deathly afraid I would experience another trigger, particularly because this was another wedding. I had considered backing out, but I knew I needed to push forward.

I decided I would prevail come what may. This time I knew what to expect and how I would feel at this wedding. I used every tool I had been taught to stave off any potential trigger.

I think seeing my business back in the black again and not having my wife in attendance had a lot to do with the victory I had over my own mind, but I was worried. I still had a jury trial that was to begin only two days later and could ill afford any setbacks. That jury trial would be the ultimate test of whether I was back in fighting form, able to bring my A-game once again.

I do not think either one of my children recognizes what I have lived through and yet they have been through a few breakups in their own rights. This was the mother lode of breakups, at least to me, and thankfully they were just as clueless about the mental mind-fuck I endured. Yet, I still credit both of my children for their persistence.

Whether intentional or not, my children dragged me out of my comfort zone; a zone I was all too eager to encase around me. I tried my darnedest to be the strong father figure I had always been and, although I thought I knew what was best for me, they unwittingly called my bet and raised me another. I think it is fair to say no one lost. We all gained, and I once again learned I could do so much more than I ever imagined only months before.

Father Knows Best was a wholesome show that aired on network television from 1954 to 1963. Despite the show's title, the lead character—the father—was less like a father and more like a friend. He was just a parent who loved his kids. His family absolutely came first.

Although that show predates me by a few years and I never saw it in real-time, I see a lot of similarities between the title character, Jim Anderson, and me. I named this chapter Father Knows Best as a twist of irony. My children actually knew best. Sometimes we as parents need to step away from our roles as parents and listen to our children. We can learn a lot from them if we are open-minded enough to hear what they are saying and follow their lead.

CHAPTER 15

PARSLEY SAGE ROSEMARY AND THYME

E veryone in my generation is bound to know the song *Scarborough Fair* performed by Simon and Garfunkel in 1966. It turns out the lyrics predate Simon and Garfunkel by hundreds of years to the medieval period in England. The actual Scarborough Fair took place in Scarborough, Yorkshire, England. It was a marketplace where vendors traded their wares. The fair also attracted food vendors and entertainers.

Most people, regardless of generation, are probably familiar with Parsley, Rosemary, and Thyme. They are herbs used for cooking. Sage is also an herb used in many Mediterranean dishes, but it also has medicinal qualities. The other spices are believed to have similar qualities when combined in a sort of potion or concoction, but ironically, the one herb I have heard more about now above all others is Sage.

Sage is used to rid a place of negative energy. The ancient practice of saging a home or office means burning it within the structure to allow rooms to fill up with smoke. Smoke is thought to ward away negative forces and replace those forces with healing energy.

To date, I have yet to meet a solitary divorced man who has spoken to me about the benefits of saging a home and yet divorced women seem to know all about it. I think I know what that says, but I will spare my kindred spirits the cold, hard truth.

My ex-wife and I were cordial to one another, and I never felt like my home was filled with negative energy, although as I think about it, how could it not be? I spent so much of our past year bickering, crying, resenting, and begrudging those forces had to be present.

A woman I met on a dating app introduced me to sage and its benefits. She convinced me to sage my house to get a fresh start. She gave me a bundle of white sage that I was to burn inside the house. I just never got around to it, and I left the sage sitting on the bookcase in the family room. My wife saw it during the time she was at the house for a wedding and asked what it was. I was a bit tight-lipped so as not to offend her, but I had every intention to sage the house at my earliest opportunity.

When I was selling the house on Cedar Road, I knew it was time to bring in the big guns. Kelli and my realtor, Nichole, knew everything there was to know about sage and they agreed to rid the house of all the negative energy prior to the first open house. I can only imagine what that poor house went through with Don and the goons inside.

Kelli once told me she felt sorry for the house. She described it as a house wanting desperately to be a home. I never thought about it like that, but I completely understood. A house can be a refuge for its inhabitants, or it can possess bad energy. A house can bring about tranquility or it can be a reminder of certain horrors.

Kelli and Nichole went into the house armed with sage and crystals. I remained out of the home. I could not bring myself to enter, as it would very definitely set back my healing process. The house I once took such pride in became nothing but a sore subject.

I later got the report from Kelli that the house was thick with negative energy. She knew nothing about who slept where, but as she saged, the powerful negative forces were fighting to remain. Kelli described forces of evil and contempt that gradually diminished as they continued the cleansing process.

Kelli could tell me without any prior knowledge whose room had the most powerful negative energy. After an exhausting day of saging, she and Nichole went home to rest. They told me certain parts of the house needed a second round of sage and they went back the next day to complete the job. I finally gathered the strength to enter the house but only after being assured it was clear of the evil, demonic, and petulistic forces that once resided there. I could feel and smell a healthy calmness about the house.

Kelli and Nichole have promised to sage my office, a place that had been home to extremely negative forces from clients who have come in for everything from robbery to rape. I have no idea how much of this negative energy has permeated my soul.

I only know when I finally dared to walk into the house on Cedar Road after it had been saged, I felt a tranquilness I had not felt at any point. The air smelled crisp, and I was able to walk around the house at peace, knowing this house now had a fighting chance to become the home it was destined to be. Feeling this amazing transformation has made it even more imperative that I sage my office.

On the weekend of the open house, people were lined up outside. Within two days, I had four offers, all for above the asking price. At one point in my life, that house represented something of significance. As time went on, I was able to glance over at the house as I drove by and dream about its possibilities. Finally, I was at peace with everything about that house and knowing it would soon become a home made me happy.

CHAPTER 16

MARA MARA ON THE WALL, WHO O' WHO IS ON THIS CALL

One woman who has been near and dear to me is my friend Mara (pronounced Mær-uh). I met Mara on a dating app. I must have given her my cellphone number at some point because she called me suddenly while I was lying on the couch, probably listening to tear-jerking ballads.

This is where the story takes a very funny and unusual twist. Her voice is identical to another Mara (pronounced Mair-uh), who is a prosecutor. When she merely identified herself as Mara and I heard her voice, my mind immediately went to prosecutor Mara, not Bumble Mara.

Thinking Bumble Mara was Prosecutor Mara, I was extremely unguarded. The conversation was as real as it gets. I have known prosecutor Mara for many years, and we have had countless cases together. She has always had a very sweet disposition and has been an extremely professional prosecutor who always treated my clients and me fairly. I did not always agree with everything she asked the judge to do in court, but she has her job to do, and I have mine. Ours was a collegial relationship, so I was not caught off guard that she might be calling me on my personal cellphone.

I was doing my usual cursing and complaining about cases and clients dropping F-bombs every other phrase with whom I thought was prosecutor Mara and Bumble Mara went right along with it. We spoke for nearly an hour, and I talked about cases we had together, and I am certain we talked about my marital separation.

To Bumble Mara, the conversation ebbed and flowed in such a way that certain topics were relatable and sounded like the topics appropriate for Bumble while others were clearly in the criminal law litigation vain. But Bumble Mara continued to listen and engage me, thinking all the while what she perceived as my incoherence may have been a sign of severe mental illness brought about by my marital woes. At a minimum, she viewed me as someone who needed counseling.

Approaching the end of the hour, I must have said something like *see you in court*. She finally asked me who it was I thought I was talking to. I matter-of-factly answered prosecutor Mara, except I used her complete name. It was only then she identified herself and we both realized the conversation was one big misunderstanding. We laughed uncontrollably once we both realized who was whom.

It turns out Mara works in the pharmaceutical industry and several of her prescription medications are designed to help people with mental health disorders. We spent roughly another hour dissecting our conversation from beginning to end, laughing all the while about the parts that made no sense to someone who was not a prosecutor.

She told me she let our conversation go on because in between the litigation parts were enough general topics that made sense, but she also told me the thought crossed her mind to recommend some of the medications she provides. This really was one of the funniest things that ever happened to me, and it happened at a time when I needed a good belly laugh.

Mara and I never personally met and yet I count her as one of my dearest friends. I never really thought about having a *pen pal* who lives only an hour and a half away, but Mara has always checked on me at times when I desperately needed. I want to think I have done the same for her. She must have a sixth sense.

We have both been through a lot in our personal lives and we trust each other implicitly because of the brutal honesty and sincerity that began the night we mistakenly laid our souls bare. When on-line dating scammers and catfish seemed ubiquitous, Mara was (and still is) a breath of fresh air.

During one of our many conversations, I learned she had spent her early childhood in the very town inhabited by my wife's family. This is the town my wife moved to when she left me. What are the odds? I also learned about the breakdown of her marriage, and she learned a lot about mine. Because of the way we met, we skipped all the games and the pleasantries and got right down to the se-rious topics concerning life after divorce.

Mara has been a close confidant and friend who I can trust with my deepest, darkest secrets and I believe she feels that way about me. With Mara, there is never any pretense. I often turn to her for the unbridled truth from the female's perspective. Likewise, when she wants the male perspective, I give it to her with brutal honesty.

None of these truthful conversations would have felt so natural or happened so quickly had I not made the mistake I made. She knew who I was, but I sure as hell did not know who she was. Even a mistake of identity like the one I made can be a blessing in disguise.

I am also grateful to Mara's contemporaneous review and recommendations concerning this book and I feel honored to be writing this important chapter about our special relationship. Not only is she a valued friend, but she is a gifted editor whose advice I welcomed.

Additionally, she continues to confide in me about the changes taking place in her life, from the recent sale of her marital home to her new abode. She appears to be getting her life on track, and I am ecstatic about that. I also appreciate how she has taken a hard look inward after reading parts of the book and has taken on board my call for changes in the way we treat each other on an everyday basis.

One of my many goals in writing this book was to make people think about how we treat others going through difficult, life-altering changes. She recently told me she reached out to a friend of hers to give her encouragement and that she may not have if she had not read certain parts of this book. Nothing makes me happier than to know someone has read my writing and then decided for herself to make a change. The change will not happen overnight, and change is almost always met with resistance, but it can take place even if it happens one person at a time.

CHAPTER 17
SPECIAL K

The dry-cleaning service I used the most was located only three doors down from my office. The facility was a matter of convenience, and they did a reasonably good job. In an ultimate twist of irony as a Special Assistant United States Attorney, I had conducted a Grand Jury investigation into the practices of the former dry cleaner at the same location. I was attempting to determine whether violations of certain pollution statutes had taken place there.

The Environmental Protection Agency had already taken soil samples and discovered that dry-cleaning chemicals had permeated the soil. I inherited that investigation from another Assistant United States Attorney, so I do not recall how that dry cleaner ever got onto the EPA's radar, but after sample results came back, it was determined that a carcinogenic chemical had been dumped near the building.

The real questions were who dumped them, when, why, and whether that dumping was intentional. I concluded my investigation and could not file any indictments because no one seemed to know anything about those chemicals, at least that they were willing to discuss.

I had been dropping my clothes off at the dry-clearer for years and was always met by a pleasant person named Kelli. (Yes, the Kelli who saged my house.) She was always attentive, sweet, kind, and extremely efficient at what she did. I was usually outgoing, so it was normal for me to engage Kelli in a little light-hearted banter.

At some point, I must have brought up what I did and where I worked. When her family members needed a lawyer, Kelli recommended me. That was really the start of a true friendship that is stronger today than it has ever been.

I found that whenever I went to pick up or drop off my garments, Kelli and I engaged in some idle chitchat, even more so once the legal matters were involved. At the front of the store sat an old wooden pew I used to sit on to hold our little *prayer service* of sorts. I talked about my life, and she talked about hers. We mostly talked about matters germane to her family. I found it most satisfying to know she trusted me implicitly and knew I would do everything I could to help her family.

After a while, Kelli and I sort of hit it off. We talked about almost anything and so it was natural to bring up what was going on in my personal life, especially regarding my failed marriage. Kelli also trusted me with some of the most painful details of her life. I realized that although our stories were quite different, we were both dealing with traumas in our lives.

Kelli had my cell phone number because anytime laundry was ready for pickup, she sent out a text message. Eventually, she used that number to discuss her personal life, and I found myself not only dropping off my laundry but attending a *prayer vigil on the pew*. Other customers usually joined in on the joke and we all had a good laugh about the little one-stop-shop—a dry cleaner and church all in one convenient location.

Throughout our interaction, I learned Kelli was an empath—she could feel what others feel. She quickly locked onto me and could gauge my mood.

At first, I was skeptical. I heard about psychics, mediums, and empaths before, but I had never met one in person. My skepticism quickly eroded when I went to the dry cleaner, and she began telling me things about my deceased mother. These were details no one should have known, even the best internet sleuth. She could even tell when I was having a good or a bad hour. I knew this because she texted me and asked whether I was okay, often at the precise time I was not okay. She could describe how I was feeling to a T.

I was convinced she could tell me about myself, but I had no idea the reverse would also be true. I only remember driving along and out of the clear blue, I experienced a sudden overwhelming bout of anxiety. For reasons I still do not understand, I looked at the clock in my car and precisely observed the time I began feeling it.

Unbeknownst to me, Kelli's dog had passed away and as I was consoling her about her dog, I also mentioned how I felt burning anxiety. She asked me about when I felt it and I told her. She then sent me a text message that was date stamped at the exact same minute I felt the unexpected anxiety. I am not an empath, but I can see now how humans have the capacity to feel what others feel if we care enough to pay attention to our own feelings.

Kelli has been there for me when I had no one else in my life. One night, I was having a terrible time battling the demons in my head. I felt the walls closing in around me and wondered what I would do if the walls completely shut. I was lying in the dark and reached for my cellphone. The iPhone can pin people you text the most at the top of the screen and I knew Kelli's placement was in the upper right. I never knew anything about pinning someone into the chat and I know I never intentionally pinned her, but she was there, thank God.

Not knowing who to turn to for help and feeling my vision deteriorating, I reached for my cellphone, and tapped on the upper right portion of the screen. Kelli answered, as she always did. I told her what I was feeling, and she walked me through it until I felt it was safe to hang up with her. I honestly have no idea what was happening to me except that it felt nearly identical to the time I took Seroquel.

I feel like Kelli saved my life that night by just being a voice in the dark who reassured me everything was going to be alright. I could literally call Kelli day or night and she was always there and never asked for anything in return. This is precisely what I meant by guardian angel. I think God put Kelli in my life to protect and guide me when even some of my closest friends and family members were AWOL.

I arrived at the title Special K because my friendship with Kelli is special indeed. She ensured I had a home cooked meal once a week by spending her entire day each Sunday cooking for me and even my dog Oscar. I am reminded of my brother Mike's expression that to have a friend, one must be a friend.

Kelli may be the rare exception to that rule. She has done far more for me than I have ever done for her. Even when I offered to pay her for all the food she prepared, she refused to take it. Her gifts are truly from her heart, and she does those things with no expectation of receiving any benefits or compensation in return. The text message below is typical of the sort of thing Kelli would send me just to let me know she cared.

Pardon my intrusion... i just wanted to tell u that I'm so fuckin proud of u.....For pushing through all the mess no matter how hard it was at times... For building resilience and strength every single time u got back up after a long and treacherous fall...For getting up every fuckin day despite the heaviness that had settled in ur heart.... For having the courage to persevere through the storm....For holding on to the hope that something better is awaiting u on the other side....

For continuing to cradle that hope when everything around u was unknown.... Thats fuckin bravery... And unbridled courage... and that is something worth being very proud of....selfishly i hope u always need ur "security blanket" 😘 *...cause this adventure called life is so much better with u in it* 🤍 *That is all .... as u were* 😌

Kelli always talked about law. She later told me she was fascinated with trial work and was fixated on litigation, police interrogations, and investigations. I could feel the planets aligning and as soon as the opportunity presented itself, I brought Kelli onboard to work with me. She has been an incredible new addition to my office and has been incredibly well-received by clients.

Kelli has enriched my life like few I have met. I not only have a secretary who is incredible, but I have a friend who cares deeply for me and my well-being. As humble as Kelli is, I am sure she would not accept the title of guardian angel, but that is how I see her, and that is the lesson here. Be receptive enough to embrace people who are willing to make themselves a part of your life without asking for anything in return.

Even as I write this, Kelli has been one of my biggest supporters. She has multiple draft copies of this book adorning her home and she has supported my efforts like few others.

As I may have stated multiple times throughout this book, I believe God puts certain people in your life at just the right time. We may not understand why and how that happens, but if we are to only have faith and trust, God will do the rest.

CHAPTER 18

MI AMOR

One day I received a text from a woman, Judyth, who lived in Petersburg, Virginia. Judyth was a Latina, originally from Ecuador. My middle brother frequented Cuba several times a year and married a Cuban woman. That relationship ended in sorrow, and she eventually died of cancer at the age of 38. As I referenced in a prior chapter, his love story—their story —is filled with unspeakable grief and tragedy and could be the subject of a book or movie. But that story is for him to tell when (or if) he is ready to tell it.

He often told me a lot about Latin American culture and how the people were always warm and happy despite having few material possessions and practically no money. La Familia—family—was the number one thing in their lives, not work, success, belongings, and money. My brother often told me if I ever met a Latina I would understand.

I decided to give this relationship a chance. I checked out all seven or eight of Judyth's profile pictures and found that her smile glowed like the northern lights. If a smile is the gateway to the soul, my eyes were the MRI. I saw everything about her in high definition and in technicolor. Having just been scammed, I was nervous to give any personal information to another woman, but something about Judyth seemed different.

We briefly texted, and I gave her my cellphone number just in case she ever wanted to call me. I was always skeptical of going to third-party sites, especially after having been scammed, but something about her made me relax my guard. Had she truly wanted to scam me, she had me in a vulnerable position. I downloaded the WhatsApp app and did not give it another thought.

Around January 2022, I had flown to visit my daughter in Nashville. I was in full-blown depression mode, but I fought through it to see my daughter. As much as I thought about suicide, I did not really want to go through with it.

I am ashamed to admit, I prayed that our plane would crash so I could be free of the burden I carried and that none of it would be my fault. I realize now that was an extremely selfish prayer, but at that moment, I was fixated only on myself and my problems. I even Googled how to kill myself and make it look like an accident. Looking back on it all now, I cannot believe I ever felt that despondent, but I did.

I was ever grateful to my daughter for inviting me to Nashville and, as depressed as I was, I tried my best to hide it from her. I had the best time I could under the circumstances. My daughter was so incredibly understanding and gave me space when I needed it.

I think she knew the state of my mind, but we never openly discussed it. Only once did she tell me I seemed sad and not like my usual self, but she had been through a few breakups herself and understood mine was no ordinary breakup.

Again, she was the best hostess she could have been, even giving up her bed to me and sleeping on the couch. I tried hard to be the best dad and guest I could. Nothing was easy then, but I think her own experiences with relationships gave her insight into what I might have been feeling.

One day while sitting in a bar, I received a video on WhatsApp. The video was from Judyth. She was in Ecuador for three weeks to visit her family. Her video was so sweet and sincere and was in perfect English. I found out later she opted to record her video rather than to live chat so she could redo it if her English was not perfect. Unfortunately, I never got to view any of the outtakes.

When my daughter briefly left the table, I decided I would record a video of my own to send to Judyth. My video was nothing special. It was only me saying where I was and who I was with. I thanked her for her video and promised we would meet after she returned from Ecuador.

Looking back at that video now, I see a man who was ashen and devoid of any emotion. She thought the video was great at the time, but as we got to know each other, she even admitted the person in that video was not the same person she later got to know.

The funniest part about her video was her acknowledgment that she was a little fat. I found that to be funny, but not funny enough to warrant any comment. I am not the brightest guy, but I know when a woman brings up her weight, the best thing a man can do is exercise his right to re-main silent on the topic.

Anyway, it really did not matter to me. She was beautiful, youthful, and had an incredibly sweet voice and personality. Most important, she was excited to meet me, thus obliterating the paradigm I created that I was undesirable and not worthy of love.

Once she was back home from Ecuador, we com-municated often and eventually decided to meet in person. This alone was a bit shocking because most women seemed content to text *ad infinitum*. I had reserved a hotel for myself in case it was a late night in Chester, Virginia.

I was warned by my then-therapist and a few friends not to stay overnight, especially with her. The fear was I did not know who she really was. Everyone had conjured up a scenario where she would open the hotel room door while I slept to allow a couple of guys to enter. If the scenario had played out, these guys were going to club me into oblivion and steal whatever money I had.

My friend, who is also a Virginia State Trooper, told me I should take a picture of her automobile license plate in case I disappeared. That way, at least they would have a lead on the culprits. I did just that and texted him that photo. She and I laughed about that scenario as we later got to know each other, especially because she was being warned about me at the exact same time as I was being warned about her.

For some crazy reason, every time I thought about that night, I thought about the movie theater scene in the film *Malibu's Most Wanted*. In *Malibu*, the character Brad Gluckman, aka B-rad-G, a white rapper who had adopted black culture, was supposed to be scared white again. The movie theater scene was a test of whether the conversion was sufficient.

B-Rad was supposed to watch a horror movie scene and if he resisted yelling at the movie screen, he passed the test. But just as the knife-wielding killer on the big screen was about to attack the unsuspecting girl (as often happens in cheesy horror flicks), B-Rad jumped up and yelled, *Run bitch, run! He gonna kill you!* I showed a YouTube clip of that scene to Judyth and we both found it hysterical as it so closely aligned with what our friends envisioned for the both of us.

Soon after we met, my depression disappeared almost instantaneously. Judyth and I were great for each other. We had more laughs together than I can possibly count and, for the first time in a long time, I felt loved again. I also had so much suppressed love that it came pouring out as if from a sieve.

Everything seemed perfect. I was doing things around the house I had not done in years, prompting my daughter to ask, *What has this woman done to you?* It seemed no matter what we did or where we went, we always had a funny story. We were inseparable and called each other multiple times a day.

When my daughter came home, Judyth called me, and her moniker came up as Mi Amor, meaning My Love. As my phone rang later in the day, my daughter asked, *Is that Mi Amor?* That name stuck from that point and became her sobriquet.

Later that night Judyth and I were laughing and giggling on a FaceTime video for hours as we were both in our separate beds, prompting my daughter to tell me the next morning we sounded like two teenagers. At first, I was slightly embarrassed, but I realize now that was a compliment of sorts because that is how I felt—like a teenager courting my first love. We had a special relationship. Even today, my daughter asks about Mi Amor.

Soon after we met, we took a three-night trip to Fort Lauderdale. I wanted to go away with her to understand her more. The difficulty was in planning the trip. My ex-wife and I had been to so many places in Miami and Fort Lauderdale that to go to a nice hotel that was also one where I had not previously stayed required careful planning, but I found just the place.

I was still nervous with her, even though I had no reason to be. I was either so nervous or careless that I forgot to pack any extra underwear. We laughed about that before taking an Uber to Ross to buy boxer briefs, something I would never have been caught dead in when I was married.

Though Judyth gave me a new bravado, I still needed work and in a moment of complete candor, she said there was one thing I needed to work on. She used the Google translator to get it right and the English word was self-confidence. I completely understood that. My life had been ripped apart and my self-confidence decimated. But I had to show Judyth I had self-confidence.

As soon as the cleaning lady showed up to our room with more towels, I jumped out of bed donning my new boxer briefs and opened the door. The cleaning lady quickly looked me up and down and then smiled before handing me the towels. Judyth and I later laughed almost uncontrollably.

The next morning, the same cleaning lady was cleaning a room several rooms down from ours. She must have heard our voices as we exited our room and entered the hallway. Suddenly, she appeared from the room she was cleaning and loudly said, *You two have a nice day!* From that moment on, the issue of self-confidence was never mentioned.

We dated for about six or seven months before I was triggered. During that time, I traveled to Chester, or she traveled to Chesapeake. She had been in two serious automobile accidents in Ecuador. In one, her car rolled over multiple times.

Naturally she was fearful about driving, but throughout our relationship she gained the courage to drive from her house to mine, a one-hour and forty-five-minute transit. I was as proud of her for conquering her fear as she was of herself.

I will always remember Valentine's Day 2022. I had made a reservation on the website Open Table for a very nice steak house in the Shockoe Bottom district of Richmond, Virginia. We both dressed up and got to the restaurant on time. I told the hostess I had a reservation and gave her my name, to which she replied, I see no such reservation. I said there must be a mistake; I had the text to prove it.

She asked to look at it and, as soon as she did, she said that the reservation was for the following Tuesday. I am not sure how that happened, but I was embarrassed beyond belief. Like the great sport she always was, Judyth shrugged it off, and we enjoyed our Valentine's Day dinner while sitting at the bar.

Once we went out in a boat and had the time of our lives. My boat is a 26-foot Chaparral bow rider I bought when my family was battling Covid-19. We needed an escape from the social distancing and the quarantine, and the boat offered the perfect solution. When Judyth and I went out on the boat, the boat seemed like a little slice of paradise. We had the music cranking and were free as birds. She describes that little boat adventure as her most favorite summer memory. I am so proud of that.

One of the funnier moments was when I let her steer the boat and I was busy doing deckhand stuff. I pointed in the direction we needed to cruise and told her to just *hold'er steady*. I looked no further until suddenly, she started crying out, *baby, baby, baby*!

I quickly looked at our course heading and realized we were dangerously close to running aground on a little peninsula surrounded by shoal water. I grabbed the steering wheel and corrected our heading. We and the boat were never really in any danger, but we still laughed about that moment.

For a time, we were inseparable. I found it interesting that although we came from two different worlds and spoke two different languages, we always understood one another. She understood my dry sense of humor and I understood hers. I saw a bright future with her, even though she was the first woman I had been with in any meaningful way since my separation.

Unfortunately, when my life came crashing down around me because of triggers and stress, I lost her. I pushed her away because I tried to spare her the misery of my life as it unraveled. What I thought was a noble gesture turned out to be a decision I will always regret.

She had opened her life to me. Particularly, she opened her home and her family to me. She also exposed me to Latin American culture, cuisine, and music. I began trying my hardest to learn Spanish. My goal was to speak with her and her family in their native tongue.

I recall vividly the very moment I destroyed our relationship. It was one of my saddest days. Lying next to her on her bed, I tried to explain my life and its complexities. I explained how I was trying my darndest to restore order to the chaos—to re-assemble the shattered pieces of my life. I am not sure why or how I came up with this expression, but I described parts of my life as needing to be organized—to be put in a box—so I would not have to deal with them.

As articulate as I could be at times, the notion of putting things in boxes was simply the wrong analogy. She took my statements as meaning I found a box—a home if you will—for every aspect of my life, but had no box for her. Nothing was further from the truth, and I did an extremely poor job of convincing her otherwise. I hurt her deeply and, in the process, hurt myself. Anyone who may not realize how words have consequences only needs to talk to me about this epic blunder.

After our official breakup, Judyth told me she needed space to clear her mind. I respected that until I realized she was as infatuated with me as I was with her. Ours was a special relationship and some unknown force kept drawing the two of us together. We were now both riding an emotional rollercoaster.

I was trying with all my might to recover and felt I only needed additional time to get myself back to full strength. In retrospect, I wasn't being fair to her, but I was doing the best I could. However, time ran out when Judyth informed me our relationship needed to end. It was taking too much of a toll on her. I know I hurt her deeply and couldn't blame her.

I knew desperate times often called for desperate measures and, being a movie buff, I thought of two great romantic movie scenarios. The first was *An Officer and A Gentleman* and the other was *Jerry Maguire*. Both movies had unexpected romantic endings where the leading men surprised the leading women and they all supposedly lived happily ever after.

I had conjured up a hybrid movie scene where I would show up at Judyth's place of employment and carry her out of the warehouse where she worked as in the closing scene to *An Officer and A Gentleman*. I would then tell her how much I loved her, how good we were for each other, and then promise to take care of her for the rest of my life. I expected her to tell me to shut up; I had her at hello as in *Jerry Maguire*. The stage was set in my mind.

I drove the entire trip north, listening to all the ballads we had shared together. Most of them were in Spanish, but the melodies were simply incredible, and an unmistakable passion emanated from the voice of the Spanish singers known to Judyth and me. Most notably, I fell in love with the uniquely raspy Andalusian sound of Alejandro Sanz's voice. I played his music over and over as I was prone to do getting more excited with each passing mile.

As I got closer and closer to her place of employment, the anticipation was building. Sanz and one other Spanish singer—Pablo Alboran—provided the perfect soundtrack to the movie I conjured up in my head. I finally pulled into the parking lot around 12:30 p.m. and noticed her car pulling in just ahead of me.

Phase one of my plans was already busted, as the notion she would see me from across the warehouse and run into my arms or that I would pick her up and carry her out were now impossibilities.

But I improvised and excitedly parked next to her car and got out to greet her.

It was at that moment I realized her son was driving her car, not her. But phase one still seemed viable because I believed she was inside. I exited my car and greeted her son, only to learn she was not inside. She had taken the day off and was somewhere in the Shenandoah Mountains hiking with her daughter.

Now the reality hits me that not only was phase one shot all to hell, but phase two as well. My movie script, complete with a Latin-American and Spanish soundtrack, had gone completely belly up. As I drove home, I could only think to myself, *fuck Richard Geer and Tom Cruise, fuck Hollywood and all romantic movies*. I put country music on the radio and drove home, feeling deflated.

Day after day, week after week, I sat in my car listening to the ballads we enjoyed, most of which were in Spanish. On several occasions, I arrived at the gym with the intention of working out, only to sob openly as I thought about the person I lost and the love I killed. Often, I never even went inside the gym, but cried until my tears dried up and drove home to cry some more.

These are only a few stories that illustrate our relationship. This book could be filled with hundreds more, most of which are too private to share. We never went anywhere or did anything that did not result in at least an emotional or funny story. I was sillier and goofier than I had been in years, and that is saying something because, as my children will attest, I have always acted far younger than my chronological years.

I believed God put Judyth in my life for a reason and a season. Several people were praying for God to bring a good woman into my life, and I was convinced Judyth was that woman. I texted *A* and a few other prayerful friends about Judyth. I sent them a few pictures of her as well.

A was ecstatic as he told me, *Bro... bro, this is exactly the woman I saw in my dreams. She's your queen, bro.* He described the woman in his dream as having the same olive-colored complexion and reddish hair. I needed no more convincing.

One of the most impressive things about Judyth is that she had read the Bible cover to cover. Her Bible is highlighted, and notes are scattered in the margins throughout. I later learned she obtained her undergraduate degree in theology. I honestly desired to read the Bible from cover to cover, but during every attempt, I begin with Genesis and find the passages to be a bit too confusing and give up. My goal is to read the entire Bible someday, specifically, the Original Authentic King James or earlier versions.

One thing that made an indelible impression on me was Judyth's willingness to attend Catholic Mass at my parish. In the last few years of my marriage, I tried to be a little more physical with my wife. I would put my hand on her leg as we listened to the homily, hoping I was speaking her love language and hoping she would reciprocate by placing her hand on my leg. I can't say I blame her, but that never happened.

But with Judyth, I always felt an incredible warmth and knew we spoke each other's love language without ever uttering a word. I had my hand on her leg and she had her hand on mine. It felt so natural. There is something about listening to the Holy Gospel and homily while touching Judyth that seems to cause the message to permeate even deeper into Mi Corazon (my heart).

Judyth and I were incredibly good for each other and had I not been subjected to mental jiu jitsu that led to my ultimately pushing her away for what I thought were noble reasons, I believe we would still be together. But I will always love her and be grateful to her for teaching me so much about life and love. I will always hold her close to my heart and be her special friend until I take my last breath. She is an incredibly special woman and the man who ends up with her will be blessed beyond measure.

CHAPTER 19
A JURY OF MY PEERS

Tuesday, October 11, 2022, was the day I dreaded the most, and it was also the biggest test of my recovery. This was the case that would either mark my new beginning or signal the end of my career.

Could I meet the most basic standards of competency expected of any licensed practicing attorney? Would I perform up to the high standard I not only set for myself but was expected of an attorney with my years of experience and expertise? Only time would tell.

What made this case so problematic was that I had convinced myself I no longer wanted to be an attorney. I was convinced I was incapable of staying focused long enough to timely object, make cogent persuasive arguments, and carry out some semblance of order in conducting the case. I had no idea how I would do because the matter that still stuck out in my mind was the assault case where I was triggered and that ended with the bailiff yelling *order in the court.*

I had also done a few prior pretrial motions hearings where I felt my mind was so blocked that I would get stuck on a particular word and then repeat it over again as if that was the only scholarly word in my vocabulary. I remember it well. The word I used was labyrinthine and I must have used it in my oral argument ten times.

I was the fourth and final attorney assigned to this case. In the six years this case languished, the original prosecutors came and went as well.

The allegations were that my client and his cohort broke into and entered a garage adjacent to a house where he found an elderly man. Allegedly, he pistol-whipped the man, dragged his bloody body into his own house and, after ransacking the house, made off with the man's wallet and a few other items.

The Sixth Amendment to the U.S. Constitution states in pertinent part, *in all criminal prosecutions, the accused shall enjoy the right to a speedy trial.* However, any delay attributable to the accused does not count toward speedy trials.

For example, if the accused's attorney withdraws from a case or the accused fires his existing attorney and his actions cause the delay, that delay does not count against the prosecution for speedy trial purposes. What no one could foresee was that when Covid struck, court activities, including jury trials, were halted and suspended the Constitutionally guaranteed right to speedy trial. In other words, a mere executive order issued by a governor effectively killed the Sixth Amendment.

To make matters worse for those caught in the crossfire of the Covid pandemic, the Supreme Court of Virginia issued its own order, suspending speedy trial rights. To be clear, the federal judicial system operated on an even stricter set of orders, particularly suspending habeas corpus and leaving an accused with nowhere to turn for redress. A person held pretrial without bail during Covid was just shit out of luck.

After six years of waiting, two of which were due to Covid and the subsequent executive and court orders, we were a mere two days away from trying the case when several witnesses announced they had Covid-like symptoms. The judge, unwilling to risk a mistrial due to jury illnesses caused by those witnesses and not wanting to be responsible for hosting a super-spreader event, made the decision to postpone the trial once again. My client was forced to wait another six months before finally having his day in court. I felt bad for him, but I was thinking those six months might have been the time I needed to get back into fighting form.

When the first day of the jury selection finally arrived, I knew I would have to stand before sixty-five or so potential jurors (veniremen as they are called) and then whittle that group down to twelve, the minimum number of jurors required for a criminal jury. To reduce the entire group (the venire) from sixty-five to twelve, the judge, the prosecution, and the defense engage in a process called *voir dire*, which etymologically means to speak the truth.

During this process, the judge asks a series of questions of the venire to expose any biases an individual may have either for or against the prosecution or the defense. The prosecution then gets to ask its questions and finally, the defense asks its questions. The court brings in individuals one by one for individual voir dire to avoid biasing the entire venire and prevent embarrassment to a specific venireman. During this process, both sides can ask specific questions about an answer given in response to a more general question.

For example, if a question is asked whether anyone had been the victim of a violent crime or knows someone who has, those answers would be better disclosed in the more private setting involving only the judge, the lawyers, the clerk, the court reporters, the bailiffs, and, of course, the accused.

If either side believes a particular venireman cannot be fair and impartial, the attorney can move to strike that person for cause. After all the veniremen are struck for cause, each side gets a certain number of peremptory challenges. This means that, notwithstanding a few exceptions, a potential juror can be struck for any reason or no reason at all. Sometimes, a venireman is struck based solely on a gut feeling.

Other times, a peremptory challenge is used to strike a person whom the attorney believes should have been struck for cause, but the judge ruled otherwise. The ultimate goal is to select twelve people who are fair and impartial, and once chosen, they are sworn in as the jury.

I had done more jury trials than I can count, but this was much different because this jury trial was the first in nearly three years. This one was the first to follow my separation and its concomitant depression, anxiety, and complete loss of self-esteem.

Some people have an intense fear of public speaking and I suppose I did too in the beginning of my career, but after twenty-five years, I gained an incredible amount of self-confidence. I used to say it was the Robert Wegman show whenever I did a jury trial. I believed I had the right personality and charisma to persuade a jury that there was a reasonable doubt.

In the criminal litigation business, getting the jury to like you bolsters your credibility and gives you greater odds of winning the case for your client. But to borrow an expression from my late father-in-law, sometimes you can't turn shit into Shinola. In other words, pesky, inconvenient, and unanticipated facts can sometimes ruin a good case.

I believe I had an uncanny ability to spin bad facts into better ones and if, after I deliver my impassioned closing argument, a jury still reached a finding of guilt, I jokingly wondered whether they listened to anything I said. My feeling was if they listened to me they would have no choice but to acquit my client. Some might call that arrogance, but it is just a bravado a criminal defense attorney must possess if he is to have any hope of persuading a jury.

Surprisingly, on October 11, 2022, I felt a sense of serenity come over me, perhaps because I was so eager to get the trial started and to get it over with. This had been the one major thing looming over my head when I was at my worst and whenever I thought about this trial, my anxiety grew. I began questioning whether I still possessed the capacity not only to maintain minimum composure but also to stay fiercely engaged in the trial process seven hours a day for the two weeks it was expected to last.

Voir dire went off without a glitch and we picked our twelve jurors by lunchtime. I was satisfied with the jury comprised of eleven women and one man, who seemed to be receptive to my arguments and line of questioning. I entered the case with confidence, knowing that I stood a better than average chance of prevailing based on the facts.

However, as is common in most cases, I knew I would have major obstacles to overcome in order to secure an acquittal. Embarrassing myself was the persistent fear during the many months leading up to this case and throughout. I feared I would have a panic attack. I thought so little of myself and thought it would be apparent to anyone.

When I began my opening statement, I thought I should take a little pressure off by lowering the tension in the room. My opening remark was, *Well, isn't this the best-looking jury I've seen in three years?* My attempt at humor received a courtesy giggle that I think helped everyone to relax, especially me.

This jury proved a lot of things to me. It proved that even in my darkest moments, I could still rise to the occasion and do what I had the training, knowledge, and experience to do. I still possessed the qualities and the confidence to stand before a jury of my peers and deliver a comprehensive, factually correct, and impassioned opening statement and closing argument. I had the ability to divert the attention away from myself, my problems, and all I had been through to focus on someone else who stood to lose far more than I.

My client was ultimately convicted of six charges and acquitted of two. Several months after his formal sentencing, my client wrote to me from prison and told me I will always have his loyalty. That meant the absolute world to me. Recently he called my office, but I was not there. The message was he just wanted to check on *[his] family*. Again, these are the little intangibles that make all the stress and anxiety worth it in the criminal defense business.

The takeaway is something I have quoted throughout this book: *Never give up; never ever give up*. I have since done another jury and although the verdict was not in my client's favor, my performance was on point, and I did not feel the need to take any medications prior to or during any stage of the trial. For the first time in one and a half years, I felt like I was back to my original fighting form again.

However, as Kelli often reminds me, the original me does not exist anymore. The new me vibrates on a higher frequency. She is right, things that used to bother me no longer do. I am also able to read people and avoid those who don't uplift me, enhance my goals, or truly care about me. Those who do will find a good and faithful friend who will try his darndest not to disappoint.

CHAPTER 20
TIME HEALS ALL

I had always been told to hang in there; things would get better or it only takes time. The trouble is no one tells you how much time. When I met Judyth, my life seemed complete. What I failed to realize is I had never dealt with my trauma, I merely masked it. This was my undoing.

For those of you who skimmed over the preceding chapters and are curious about the trauma, let me fill you in. I would never claim that my life is any better or any worse than anyone else's. I fully recognize countless people's lives have been struck with unthinkable tragedies.

While discussing my writing with a few acquaintances, I learned about many horrible things in their lives, from cancer to depression and everything in between. I began asking myself what gave me the right to tell my story, especially when so many others have endured so much worse. I am no one special—trust me.

The answer is whether my story is more captivating, compelling, or spellbinding than anyone else's is immaterial. I have the right to tell my story because I know many people, including my younger brother Scott, who have killed themselves over far less. If any one person can identify with my story and it gives them hope, I am happy about that. At a minimum, writing became my therapy and my voice, and I am finally at peace.

The remaining chapters are designed to be about hope—hope for people similarly situated. In many respects, I want those chapters to be a guide to success, and I want them to open some eyes. I have heard it said that everyone is going through something and no doubt that is true. As I said in the beginning, I would like to engender some discussion or at least create some introspection about how we can make a better world for ourselves and those around us.

I would like to see people apply what Coach V said only two months away from death by cancer. He said to live each day trying to do three things—laugh, cry, and think. He went on to say if you live every day doing just those three things, you have had a hell of a day. I could not agree more and have followed Coach V's advice throughout my journey.

Coach V also admonished us to *never ever give up*. As much as I wanted to give up, I did not, and you should not either. I realize now no one can forecast how long it will take for any individual's recovery, but if you fight like hell for yourself and your family; challenge yourself; stay committed to prayer; stay physically fit to the extent possible, and laugh, cry, and think, your chances exponentially increase.

In short, if you do all or some of those things whether, consecutively or concurrently, you will have heeded Coach V's proposition to never give up. You will have had no choice.

CHAPTER 21

OBJECTION COUNSELOR

My wife and I thought going to a counselor at Catholic Charities would really help us. We were looking for a counselor who understood Catholicism and Christianity. We were hoping to get counseling from a Biblical perspective. If Father Jack had been around, I think my marriage could have been saved, but she had her counselor and I had mine.

Later, we committed an unforced error by going to my counselor instead of someone fair and impartial. My counselor had gotten a heavy dose of my spin on our marital woes and was prone to taking my side, and that deeply offended my wife.

She finally unloaded on the counselor by telling her I was the one in the wrong and the counselor was jaded and duped into thinking I was the one getting shafted. We quit after that and never looked back.

The other time I went to counseling, I had been given a referral to see a counselor through one of the hospital systems. This counselor sat quietly while I talked for the entire hour. She never interrupted me or even challenged some of my thoughts and conclusions. I got the feeling that once she learned I was an attorney, she was intimidated by my career status. But I was not going to her as an attorney, but as a broken man who needed her help.

I once made the statement to my hospital counselor that I was doing all the talking and was told that is what I was supposed to do. But I was looking for more than that. I was looking for coping skills and words of encouragement. My counselor provided none of those things.

I quit seeing that counselor after only three or four visits. I suppose that is another reason why I was hesitant to continue with counseling. I never had a good experience and was not at all looking forward to rehashing the same old backstory with yet another counselor.

My former secretary recommended a counselor who was trained in the use of Eye Movement Desensitization and Reprocessing (EMDR). EMDR is a psychotherapy treatment designed to alleviate distress associated with traumatic memories. I was told EMDR was one of the newest and most effective techniques to help people suffering with PTSD and severe anxiety and I specifically chose my counselor because she was certified in EMDR.

I cannot speak too much about the effectiveness of EMDR because I only had an occasion to do it a few times. On that occasion, each of my hands held a vibrating apparatus. The vibration started in the right hand and then alternated between right and left. While this pattern continued, I was asked to close my eyes and describe what I saw regarding some traumatic event we had pre-discussed. As each vibration moved from left to right, my eyes, although still closed, instinctively tracked the movement of those vibrations.

From the moment I met my counselor, I knew she understood all about what I was dealing with. For the first time since I started down the slippery slope of anxiety and depression, I was finally meeting someone who did not minimize my feelings but validated them.

During my short period of dating using the dating apps, I had been told by certain women to *get over it*, *man up*, and similar things, but I often thought anyone who could get over it after only three or four months of separation from a thirty-one-year marriage had to be a psychopath. I never thought about the stages of grief and what they meant to me. If I could have gotten over it, I would have done so in lieu of the torment I put myself through for so many months.

My final counselor, Ady Shea, is a licensed clinical social worker and when we met, we had so much in common it was uncanny. I immediately felt completely comfortable discussing my life with her.

It turns out she had served in the Israeli Defense Force (IDF) and learning Krav Maga was compulsory. The IDF is the home of Krav Maga, and though I knew her skills were undoubtedly far superior to mine, at least we had that as a common denominator.

She was so friendly and thought-provoking. For the first time in my history of counseling, I found someone who would interject whenever she felt it was appropriate and listen when she needed to listen. I could not wait to see her each week just to find out what words of wisdom she would give.

Sometimes she said things I am sure seemed insignificant to her but meant the world to me. I already stated how I thought the anxiety was feeling was as noticeable as the nose on my face but, after speaking with her, I was given the confidence to know my feelings were very much safe with me. Suddenly, I did not mind interacting with other people.

I once I told her that I always felt like a fraud, as if someone would expose me at any moment. She told me that this feeling is called *Imposter Syndrome*, and I am not alone in experiencing it. It made me doubt my ability to do even the simple tasks and worsened my already shattered self-esteem.

Up to the point of my breakup, I felt I could do a criminal case in my sleep. After my breakup, and more particularly after the trigger, my confidence was shattered. I began doubting everything I had ever done and questioning whether I could prospectively do anything.

My counselor also emphasized breathing. Breathing is something we do subconsciously, an average of 20,000 times a day. Given that breathing is an involuntary function, I never considered it much. Breathing is exoteric, and I never considered its importance in overcoming anxiety.

My counselor taught me an esoteric breathing technique called 4-7-7. It involved inhaling slowly for four seconds, holding my breath for seven seconds, and slowly exhaling for seven seconds. My sense is there is no magic formula for breathing. The beauty of this exercise is one can do it anytime and anywhere. No one needs to know you are even doing it.

I found breathing alone did little to help me. I needed a bigger distraction. As much as I wanted to be free of work and its accompanying stress, work provided a place for me to go, and it gave me something else to focus on besides myself and my problems.

One of the most important things she accomplished was to stop me from tormenting myself. I needed to quit the blame game—as in blaming myself. The blame I placed on myself was really at the core of my problems. I felt like a complete failure and fraud and was beating myself unmercifully. One of the best quotes from the movie Shaw-shank Redemption is one in which one of the lead characters says to the other that life comes down to a simple choice: you can "get busy living or get busy dying." I believe Ady persuaded me as much as she could to get busy living.

CHAPTER 22
FACE FEARS

Once my wife and I made the decision to sell the beach house in Cape Charles, we tried in vain to get someone to resolve a few maintenance issues prior to the listing. The Eastern Shore of Virginia is an interesting place. People will work but usually only for people who permanently live there. I suppose they look at the rest of us as carpetbaggers who are there to steal their solitude by bringing more traffic and enjoy the amenities they have enjoyed for generations.

I saw our home purchase as a win for the town as we were infusing the capital needed to bring the town into the 21st century. Cape Charles was growing by leaps and bounds, yet the historic review board carefully maintained the charm of this little town. The Covid pandemic caused most places to come to a halt. This was particularly felt in Cape Charles where all new construction ceased and the *little town that could* remained stagnant for two years.

We bought the house with the expectation it would be our family's getaway. I always hoped the home would remain in the family and be devised to our children once we passed away. During the height of Covid, we went to Cape Charles every weekend just to break the monotony of living in Chesapeake. We tried our hardest to support small businesses, even though the locals tried their hardest to keep us away for fear of our bringing Covid with us.

Having no luck finding anyone willing to do the work to prepare the house for sale, my wife turned to me. She asked if I would go up and spackle and paint the kitchen ceiling to cover up the stain from a water leak. I was in no mental shape to do it.

First, the very idea of going back to that house, especially knowing we were now selling it, was extremely painful to me. I was deathly afraid of being massively triggered again simply by going to the house, and I attempted to avoid it at any cost.

My wife and I verbally sparred, and I resisted going to the house as forcefully as I could. She clearly did not understand the significance that house held for me. Going there had the potential to trigger negative emotions and memories for me, and I could not risk any more setbacks.

After fiercely arguing, I finally acquiesced and made the trip to do the ceiling patchwork and painting. To my surprise, I was not triggered as I had expected, and I completed the work as best I could and left soon after. I felt I had looked down the barrel of a gun and confronted my fear, which is the point of this chapter.

On one other occasion, I was practically badgered about attending a seminar for lawyers whose practice centered on personal injury. I did not want to attend because that was not my primary practice area, but also because my preference would have been to sit at home in my safe place and to not potentially expose my mental health condition. I went primarily because I needed to prove to myself that I could do all the things I had always done prior to the triggers.

Again, my fears were overblown as I sat through the three-hour seminar with no problems, and I even asked questions of the guest speaker. I did not really have any questions I could not answer myself, but my questions were really a test to see if I could conduct myself in such a manner that my anxiety would remain undetectable. I passed that test too.

I also accepted certain tasks that I knew would challenge me. In the civil law area, sometimes lawyers must travel to the site of the claim to conduct the case. For example, if the claim accrued in Chesapeake, attorneys would often have to travel from distant places.

For this reason, certain companies offer intermediary services where they match the out-of-town firm with local counsel who, for a small fee, will make an appearance to handle certain perfunctory obligations. The local counsel who decides to take the case may not know anything about the case until a day before when they download the case file. These cases can be stressful because they are usually handled alongside the lawyer's regularly scheduled docket. Additionally, the lawyer must appear before a judge with limited knowledge about the case and precisely follow instructions or potentially ruin another lawyer's case.

For several months, I rejected all the offers that came my way, but eventually I accepted a few, brought myself up to speed, and carried out my responsibilities. But I challenged myself to do these cases even knowing they would add another layer of stress to an already stressful day.

The title of the chapter is Face Fears. I have just written about three situations where I had to persist and face my fears to bounce back. I knew I needed to fight with all my might to get myself back in proper form, and to accomplish that meant I simply had to face my fears.

CHAPTER 23
FACE THE PHYSICAL CHALLENGE

From the time I was a little boy until now, I always wanted to be bigger and stronger than I was. As a young boy, I had the agility of a gazelle, but I was also a 95-pound weakling. I tried out for the junior high school football team and never gave up. I put in maximum effort only to find myself cut from the team in favor of a boy with half my agility and mental fortitude, but who was more physically stout and capable of taking the blows that would surely come from opposing teams.

I believe the coaches saw I was skilled. I could run fast, catch, and maneuver, but one good hit would likely sideline me for the rest of the season. It was frustrating to always be cut because of my size.

Anyone who went through the public school system knows being on the football team had its advantages. Football players always dated the cheerleaders and got to walk around on game days wearing their distinctive jerseys. They were truly the big men on campus. I was merely in a support role.

I was what some would call a band geek and even though I played the drums, my function was only to play whenever a good play happened on the football field and to perform at halftime. The halftime obviously fell between halves when everyone went to the concession stands. Other than band parents, most everyone else got up to use the restroom or to get food during that time. In my opinion, band members are never given the respect they deserve and yet musicians must possess both a high level of physical stamina and mental acuity.

I was always conscious about my size and my weight, which I believe propelled me to achieve a greater body mass and overall, what we used to call *cock-strength*. *Cock-strength* is the type of strength that is not obvious. Everyone knows of a wiry guy who has some sort of inner strength. From the outside, he looks unimposing, but he is never one to give up and has the stamina and inner-strength of a Brahma Bull.

Weightlifting became a passion of mine. I was determined not to revert to the skinny guy who was picked on as a young boy. But I soon realized my strength was not enough. I saw the guy with the so-called cock-strength win out over the muscle-bound guy all the time. The musclebound guy sometimes could not move his body because he was so stilted, whereas the smaller wiry guy could stick and jab and dance around the guy too big to move.

Once, when I was shopping at Home Depot and was trying to get some tile on one of the upper shelves, I asked for assistance. The employees brought over the lift they used to reach objects on higher shelves. As a safety precaution, they block off both ends of the aisle with a chain. They only needed first to clear the aisle.

One man standing in the aisle seemed oblivious to what was happening and stood staring straight ahead. Out of concern for the employee's time, I finally walked over to the man and told him the employees were waiting to get something from a higher shelf and asked if he would mind kindly stepping out of the way for a few minutes. He asked if they were retrieving something for me and I told him they were. That was when all hell broke loose.

The man lost his temper and attacked me verbally, as if I had kidnapped his child. I did not know what to make of it. I had not been in an actual street fight since I was a little boy. I really did not know how to fight, and I certainly did not know what I was capable of. So I did what most people do in that situation.

I puffed up my chest, clenched my jaw, and uttered a few choice words. My wife walked over and asked me what happened. I told her the story that ended with *that asshole would not even move out of the way*. The man then came back and asked me who I was calling an asshole.

Our disagreement basically ended there, but I felt terrible about myself. I felt very unsure of what I would have done had the man pursued the fight more and my insecurities weighed heavily on me.

At age 55, I signed up to take lessons in Krav Maga, an Israeli form of martial arts designed to end a fight before it begins. Krav Maga is fast, violent, and decisive. The basic tenet of Krav Maga is to defend oneself and offensively strike one's opponent at the same time, leaving no opportunity for an opponent to consider and execute his next mode of attack.

At age 55, I went to orientation expecting to be given a little tour of the facilities. I had no idea I would be outside on the asphalt defending myself against multiple attackers. I was the oldest person in that class by a couple decades at least. I felt myself doubled over, gasping for air and wondering what in the hell I had done to myself.

I am confident the instructor and others in the class thought this old man will never be back, but I came back and I learned fighting techniques that gave me confidence to fend off any would-be attackers, including the Home Depot crazies and the Dons of the world.

After two years of Krav Maga, I felt I had done just about every elbow strike, knee strike, inside and outside defense Krav Maga offered. The next thing I needed to address was what to do if the fight ended up on the ground. Krav Maga had a little so-called ground game, but to really learn ground techniques, I needed to learn Jiu Jitsu. I was now 57 years old and again I was the oldest in the class.

Usually, I saw people decades younger than I was sitting in the lobby waiting for their children to finish class. I got used to getting stared at as I walked past, only to bow and then enter the mat.

I still often wonder what people thought of a man my age taking class when it appeared as if I should be sitting on my deck with a cigar in one hand and a glass of brandy in the other. But I was determined to be the best I could be, not only for my age, but for any age. I was not about to let my age get in the way.

My attempt to compete with much younger opponents made me think about the line delivered by President Ronald Reagan in his second presidential debate with the democrat candidate, Walter Mondale. Reagan was asked whether he was confident he had the stamina to be president because of his age. (At the time, Ronald Reagan was one of the oldest men to run for presidential office.) During the first debate, Reagan stumbled a bit in answering that question.

During the subsequent debate, he was more prepared. When he was asked the same question about how his age might impact on his ability to serve, he came back with one of the most memorable lines of any debate. Ronald Reagan said to the moderator, *I am not going to exploit for political purposes my opponent's youth and inexperience.* That line prompted much laughter and applause from the crowd and even from Walter Mondale, but Reagan's mindset is exactly the mindset I maintained throughout my martial arts training.

In my head I was still 25 years old even though my body lets me know from time to time just how old I really was. Regardless, my nickname was 150, as in 150% because I did things aggressively and fast. I was not about to let any young bucks beat up on this old man.

One time I was grappling on the mat with a young man one quarter my age but twice my size. I simply would not let him get the upper hand. Finally, after we stalemated, he turned to me and said, *Damn, you got that old man strength.* All I ever wanted was to know the next time I was at Home Depot or anywhere I could handle my business. If I backed down, it was my choice, and not because I felt I had no other options.

As my marriage was breaking down, my wife accused me of not putting forth enough effort to correct the deficiencies in our marriage. She never really liked being home alone at night, but that was when the classes were offered.

After a brief argument, I finally agreed and told her I would quit going to the gym and quit jiu jitsu if that would make our marriage work. That did not work and when my wife ultimately left me, I was left without a gym routine and any martial arts. All the offensive and defensive moves I had done and committed to muscle memory seemed to have been lost in a flash. I was back to being that guy at Home Depot who had no training or experience.

I continued to pay for jiu jitsu classes for about nine additional months after she left, thinking I would go back at some point, but I could not muster up the desire or energy to do it. The separation had taken a toll on me and whenever I thought about going, I resisted it.

One of the best things I did for myself was to start back at jiu jitsu. I truly missed my jiu jitsu family, and I got a very nice text message from the owner telling me most of the students were glad I was back too. Just that alone made me feel accepted and further solidified my decision to resume. I was back on the mat grappling, learning, sweating, building my stamina, and improving my confidence at almost 61 years old. I had returned to doing what made me feel good and what made me feel whole.

I once said to my instructor that what he was doing was God's work. I don't think he completely understood what I meant, but to me, jiu jitsu signaled my return to normalcy. It gave me a purpose.

Gracie Jiu Jitsu offered courses from Bullyproof to Women Empowered. The courses give people the tools to use, whether confronted with a schoolyard bully, a violent spouse, or the Home Depot psychos who are itching for a fight.

I now look forward to jiu jitsu twice a week and though I have a way to go from both a technique and stamina perspective, I am once again doing what I feel confident 99% of people my age are not doing. I am taking instructions from twenty-seven-year-old instructors and grappling with people in their twenties and thirties. I have challenged myself and set my sights on my blue belt and, hopefully, many stripes to come. I will not give up until I am forced to give up because of injuries.

In my off-schedule time, I am doing cardiorespiratory and weight training. Immediately following my separation, and at age 60, I bench-pressed 280 pounds. This weight is 20 pounds less than my all-time maximum weight of 300 pounds, 60 pounds more than my body weight. I have set my goals at doing 280 pounds once again, but whether I achieve that is immaterial to me.

Weight training is personal—between the person lifting and the weight. I have discovered that everyone in the gym is supportive of everyone, regardless of the weight they lift. The general philosophy seems to be that if someone is trying to put forth an effort, it does not matter what weight they can push.

CHAPTER 24

BELIEVE

Anxiety is often the result of a poor self-esteem. Looking back on life, I had been *figuratively kicked to the curb* several times by my college girlfriend and my wife. I am certain the former event made this transition from married life to single life even harder than it had to be.

My college girlfriend was a German foreign exchange student. We met when I was a sophomore in college, and she was a freshman. She was incredibly beautiful and exotic, which was an instant attraction for me.

The first year we met, I was supposed to go visit her in Germany over the summer. I had my plane ticket and was literally teeming with excitement.

The thought of going to Europe for the first time was mind-blowing. I had never been out of the country and had barely ever been on a plane, and here I was about to travel to Germany.

A couple of days before I was to embark on my trip, I received a telephone call from her sister Karin, who told me I should not come. She said her sister had met another man who was the concertmaster of the Berlin Philharmonic Orchestra.

For those of you wondering what that means, he was the first chair violin player of one of the most prestigious orchestras in the world. Next to him, I didn't even play second fiddle. I was merely a budding percussionist whose acclaim was making the North Carolina all-state band. I decided I would go to Germany, anyway. I had convinced myself once she saw me again, the concertmaster would be history.

I saw her once I arrived in Germany, but she was enthralled with the concertmaster. I decided to make the most of my time in Germany and went to several pubs where I met one of her best friends' sister, Anna. We immediately hit it off. My girlfriend got jealous and her jealousy increased the more I spent time with Anna.

As we approached the date of our departure, she told me she was done with the concertmaster and wanted to get back together. Foolishly, I agreed to forgive her, and we resumed our relationship once we both got to college.

Everything seemed back on track until I graduated from college. I was a year ahead of her and was teaching school, so I made the trip to visit her on weekends. I was completely caught off guard when one weekend I made the trip and she was not in her dormitory.

A friend of hers came down to greet me and hit me with the news she was seeing one of the jocks in the house set aside just for jocks. I was devastated. She was the love of my life, and I had been forsaken for a second time. I think this breakup had a profound impact on my relationships and nearly all my decisions.

CHAPTER 25

MEDICATE, MEDICATE, DANCE TO THE MUSIC

Before discussing medications, I must first disclose I am not a doctor and I *do not* play one on TV. Peter Bergman, renowned for starring in soap operas, made a variation of that line famous in his 1986 Vicks Formula 44 commercial except that he played a doctor on TV. When speaking about his complete body of work as an actor, Peter once said he was probably best known for delivering that line.

Indeed, I am not a doctor, but I have personal experiences with some of the most potent psychotropic medications ever manufactured and prescribed. What I have to say about them is likely more than what a doctor could ever say unless he has first-hand experience taking them.

Just after September 11, 2001, I began my foray into the world of psychotropic medications. As mentioned in chapter five, I began seeing a psychiatrist in Virginia Beach, who diagnosed me as psychotic. I had no characteristics of psychosis from what I could tell, but he was the doctor and besides, I was in no shape to diagnose myself.

Every time I went back to see him, he increased my dosages or prescribed new medications until I was a zombie. The one I will never forget was Seroquel. I am sure this medication has its place, but I was not psychotic and did not need it.

The lesson for me is not to take a single doctor's advice, particularly a psychiatrist. Always get a second and even a third medical opinion before proceeding with any doctor's advice. Psychotropic medications are potent and can be extremely dangerous. There are reasons television commercials warn people that taking antidepressants can cause suicidal thoughts.

I went cold-turkey off those medications. I hated the way they made me feel. I was tired all the time and my sex drive was nonexistent. I know it is not advisable to go cold-turkey, but at that point I no longer cared.

I had doubled up on Clonazepam, a drug within the family of drugs called benzodiazepines. Benzos, as they are known, are some of the most highly addictive drugs on the market today. Not only are they psychologically addictive, but they are also physically addictive. People become addicted to benzos like they would crack cocaine or heroin. There is a reason they fall within the class of controlled substances: suddenly they are dangerous to take and even more dangerous to stop.

My doctor prescribed another anti-anxiety medication called Remeron. That drug just sounded bad to me. It sounded like the sort of drug given to a person living in an insane asylum, but I took it anyway. Kelli and I started calling it Red Rum (murder spelled backward as we learned in the horror movie, *The Shining*). The worst thing I could ever do when taking any drug was to read the list of side effects. Once I read them, I was bound to have all of them, even if they were psychosomatic.

Remeron gave me back my appetite and knocked me out, so I slept well throughout the night. Anyone who has ever battled acute anxiety knows sleep is the number one thing to keep the symptoms at bay. My worst days were absolutely those in which I did not get the proper amount of sleep. The only problem was the cocktail of Remeron and Clonazepam was enough to tranquilize an elephant. I woke up groggy every morning, and it took several hours for me to have my wits about me.

I did not like how these drugs made me feel. Psychotropic drug use always sets up an interesting dichotomy. The drugs made one feel less anxious and depressed, but once a person feels less and anxious and depressed, they feel they no longer need the medications. They wean themselves off or go cold-turkey, only to have the symptoms return. I always believed my condition was situational, so I never felt like these medications would be a permanent part of my medicinal regimen, but after discussing that issue with my primary care physician, he gave me the best explanation I ever heard and thereafter I did not fight being on the medications.

Some people have a natural level of the feel-good chemicals in the brain, such as serotonin, dopamine, and oxytocin. Others of us have less. That disparity is what my doctor referred to as a chemical imbalance.

Whenever a person operating with one hundred percent of these feel-good chemicals encounters a stressful event, maybe his levels are reduced by twenty percent, but still very much in the safe zone. Whereas one whose natural level is at seventy percent who encounters a stressful situation and whose level is offset by the same percentage, would be at fifty percent, clearly below the so-called safe level. The pill only balances out those levels. My attitude after that conversation was to take the pill.

We take pills to lower cholesterol. We take pills to lower blood pressure or to thin the blood or to reduce the number of platelets in the blood. In short, we take pills for just about everything. I felt like if I could take a pill to make me feel better and less anxious, that was an easy decision. I decided to take the pill and move on with my life. This is not to disparage or discourage herbal supplements. Whatever works for you, do it.

Once or twice, I did not realize I was going cold turkey. I had so many medications in various places around my sink I just did not see my antidepressant. I must have gone three or four weeks without taking it. I often thought about getting one of those weekly pill boxes, but I knew I would never be organized enough to fill it properly. I only know that after a short period I began getting sudden and unexpected one to two-second inter-vals of anxiety and brain shocks, like sparks going off in my head that were totally random.

I am not sure what made me think about that spe-cific medication, but a light bulb had switched on. I thought I had diagnosed the problem, and it turns out I was right. I did an internet search for withdrawal symptoms of that specific medication, and I realized what they decried was exactly what I had.

Every reputable website warned against going off the medication cold turkey. The proper way to get off any psychotropic medication is to ween your-self off gradually under a doctor's supervision. Anything other than that is considered unsafe.

I never intended to ween myself off and I certainly never intended to get off cold turkey. It was purely accidental, but it drove home the point that these psychotropic medications are not to be played with and it also showed me that if one can avoid them all together, in favor of a more natural rem-edy, it is advisable.

Many years ago, long about 2003, I suddenly lost my hearing in my left ear due to a condition known as—wait for it—sudden hearing loss. I had no idea at the time why this was happening to me, and I was on a search for answers.

I went to multiple ear, nose, and throat doctors and some suggested the problem could be solved or at least made more bearable if I were to get a hearing aid. I was only forty-two years old and could not conceive of wearing a hearing aid. No one could tell me why this was happening or what to do to correct the problem.

I finally stumbled across one doctor who made a diagnosis. He said what I had was otosclerosis, an abnormal hardening of the tissue in the inner ear, particularly the stapes bone. He set up the surgery, whereby my non-functioning stapes would be replaced by a titanium bone of the same size. I was going to have a stapedectomy that would finally restore my hearing.

What I never recall the doctor telling me is that the surgery itself could cause a side effect that eliminated or reduced the midrange and treble ranges of my hearing. I needed a hearing aid anyway to compensate for those losses.

My eardrum was so messed up during the surgery that any thoughts of SCUBA-diving again were sunk. I think that detail bothers me more than anything. I always thought about SCUBA-diving with my children, and I never had that chance and never will.

The reason for this story is to tell you certain psychotropic medications can themselves cause sudden hearing loss and I am reasonably certain had I weaned myself off those medications, my hearing likely would have been restored without resorting to unnecessary surgery that forever altered the hearing in my left ear.

CHAPTER 26

SEEK ASSISTANCE

L ife can be overwhelming, especially when we try to live alone. I remember when I first began my law practice as a sole practitioner, people told me how lucky I was not to have a boss. I was happy to hear I could take whatever time I wanted whenever I wanted to play golf, travel, or to just relax at home. Boy were they ever wrong.

I have never worked harder or longer than I have to run my practice. Anytime I chose to take off, I essentially close the firm. No work is accomplished; it all piles up or waits until I return.

A sole practitioner's life must be the hardest of all because unless I work, it does not get done. Time off also means missed opportunity costs. Prospective clients are usually anxious and no matter how much they try to exhibit patience, they often find another attorney who is more responsive.

During one of my low points, I was talking to Kelli about what I was planning for my full-time rental property. After we finally convinced Don to vacate, I briefly entertained the idea of renting the property again for more money, but the Don fiasco left me with such a bitter taste I no longer had the stomach for it.

The risk of having another deadbeat tenant and then dealing with the inevitable calls informing me something was broken, clogged, or leaking was simply too much. I wanted to simplify my life and decided once and for all I needed to sell.

Kelli told me she had just the person and put me in touch with a friend of hers who turned out to be the absolute best realtor I could have ever hoped for. She knew a thing or two about me because of her relationship with Kelli. I had seriously contemplated a for sale by owner to save the commission, but in retrospect that would have been a huge mistake.

Without Nichole's help, I would have been a complete basket case. I was in no mental shape to make the needed repairs, show the house to purchasers, negotiate any deals that came along, and then do all the necessary paperwork to perfect the sale. I left everything to Nichole, and she did an incredible job.

Often, we try to take on too much all in the name of saving a few dollars, because we feel we have greater control or because we feel too much self-importance. I realized I had not one but three jobs: my law practice, rental coordinator and rental manager for our beach house. The three jobs were really breaking me down.

A human can only take so much. Three jobs were fine when I was married and not dealing with those added pressures, but my life was different now and I had to accept I needed to scale back and take on far fewer tasks. Never be afraid to step back from your life and look at it from the one-thousand-foot level. You may be surprised to find out you are pushing yourself to the brink or maybe your stress level is already maxed out.

Everything is within your control. If you need help, ask for it. Also, never feel you are irreplaceable. Life and work got along just fine before you, and it will continue after you are gone. If you need a little Siesta midday, take it. Your productivity will improve because you will have the chance to rest your weary body and mind.

When I was in the Coast Guard, I got thirty days of paid leave every year. We could accumulate up to sixty days before any additional days started dropping away, unused and uncompensated. I may have used twenty days a year thinking somehow the office could not function without me. I was wrong and the day after my resignation confirmed that for me.

After I turned in my badge and completed all the checkout paperwork, I appeared back at the office and stood at the locked doors, ringing the buzzer for someone to let me gain entrance. I waited patiently for someone to let me in and, at that moment, I realized the office would get along just fine without me.

Another point is to not engage in self-aggrandizement. You may find this to be shocking, but you are not as important as you may think you are. Even the President of the United States is fungible. He is in office for four to eight years and then someone else steps up to be the Chief Executive. The country never falters, and continuity of government is maintained. When JFK was assassinated, Lyndon Johnson was sworn in as president while Kennedy's body was still being loaded into the cargo bay of Air Force One.

I regret I allowed my sense of self-importance to get in the way of time I could have spent with my family. I implore you not to make the mistake I made. Not only do you not need to control everything, but people are available to assist if you only call on them.

My realtor did a tremendous job readying the house for sale and conducting two open houses. We ended up with multiple offers and the house was under contract within two days. The sale only cost me a little commission, but so what? What I saved is immeasurable.

Ridding myself of the so-called hassle factor and the peace of mind I got from letting someone else handle my affairs was worth more than any commission I paid. I never went to the house once during the time Nichole worked to prepare it for sale and during the open houses and with electronic signatures, I could sign the contract and all other ancillary documents with a touch of my finger on my smartphone.

CHAPTER 27

PUT YOURSELF FIRST

How selfish one must be to put himself first, I thought. How dare we think of our own well-being? Well, let me say if we do not put ourselves first, no one else will. Taking care of ourselves does not mean ignoring those around us and being self-absorbed. It simply means taking care of yourself and listening to what your body is telling you.

I once had a workout partner twenty years my junior. If he called and wanted to train or workout, I felt a certain compulsion to oblige regardless of how I was feeling. I trained because I did not want to disappoint him, not because I had the overarching desire to train.

Likewise, if a client called me and said he only wanted me to handle his case because he was comfortable with me and trusted me, I gave in to his request despite my inclination not to take the case. I was not putting myself first—my mind and my body. If we fail to take care of ourselves and do what is good for ourselves, we cannot possibly be good for anyone else.

During the entire time I was separated, I heard people tell me to take the time I needed to be comfortable with myself and to learn to love myself. I was so used to relying on external sources to find love and happiness that I never really understood this concept. Later in my journey, I realized that to love someone else requires me to first love myself.

As parents, we all make sacrifices for the sake of our children. We will literally go without eating to ensure our children are properly nourished. We will spend our last dime not on ourselves, but on our children.

I am not suggesting we should affirmatively ignore others or stop doing the things that bring us joy, as in helping friends and family in whatever capacity you find is your calling. What I am saying is to stop when you feel like stopping. Say no occasionally if your mind and body are saying you need a break.

Recently, my daughter was traveling to Maryland to attend a wedding. She was supposed to take a flight here and I would drive her to Maryland. I chose this because I did not want to see her drive alone in bad weather and I also thought the time in the car would be a good bonding period.

Once her flight was canceled and rerouted, she asked if I was still going to come up to drive her back. I said no. She was a bit taken aback at my response, because in the past I would have driven her just because she asked, but I needed the weekend to decompress and to do the things I wanted to do even if they were nothing more than listening to music or sitting at a bagel shop.

She was slightly offended at first, but the sun still rose in the east the next morning and life continued. She made alternative arrangements to get here. That was a lot more sensible than my driving five hours only to turn around and drive back. I put myself first. I established boundaries that were not to be breached.

When we put ourselves first, it is because we require that time to rejuvenate, refresh, and revitalize. Putting ourselves first may seem antithetical to charity and love, but it is a recognition that we are gatekeepers of our own lives. No one controls us.

The simplest and most common example of putting yourself first is when you are on an airplane. Who has not heard the *oxygen mask* safety instruction? Oxygen and the air pressure are always being monitored. In the event of decompression, an oxygen mask will automatically appear in front of you.

To start the flow of oxygen, pull the mask towards you. Place it firmly over your nose and mouth, secure the elastic band behind your head, and breathe normally. Although the bag does not inflate, oxygen is flowing to the mask. *If you are traveling with a child or someone who requires assistance, secure your mask first, and then assist the other person.* Keep your mask on until a uniformed crew member advises you to remove it.

This is the classic example of putting yourself first. In the *oxygen mask* case, someone needs help, but to help that person, you must first help yourself. If you pass out due to the loss of cabin pressure and the absence of oxygen, not only do you potentially die, but the person needing help potentially dies as well. The concept is simple—take care of yourself first so you can be around to take care of others.

I still believe if I died in court because of a massive heart attack, some of my clients would literally nudge my lifeless body aside and then say, *Great; who is going to represent me now?* Recently, I had planned a vacation for mid-December and my clients were in court wanting a speedy trial. The judge asked if I could do it the very week I had blocked off for my vacation. I thought about it once or twice and then said I was unavailable.

As much as I wanted to help him, I had put myself first and decided he would have to wait a few more weeks until I returned. This was not just a matter of a vacation, but much needed time off to recharge my body. I was feeling burned out and needed time to get away from everything and everyone. I would be no good to him unless I could recalibrate my mind and to do that, I needed to step away from the daily grind. At that moment in court, I placed my oxygen mask firmly over my nose and mouth.

CHAPTER 28

PRAY FOR PEACE AND STRENGTH

To some, this will be a controversial topic. I am not sure why because we, as a creation, work harmoniously together and are so complex in design, it seems clear we could only have been created by a higher power. Whether one accepts this premise or believes humans evolved from primates is of little concern to me, but it does make me question why we do not have talking sea creatures and birds by now. Is evolution only reserved for humans?

I look around in wonder at all creations, not only animals. I wonder how trees know to shed their leaves in the fall and bloom in the spring; turtles know to crawl upon the sand to lay their hatchlings; and such animals as flounders, chameleons, and the Eastern Scratch Owl have all become masters of disguise? The examples are endless.

Yet whenever I get involuntarily trapped in the atheists' and agnostics' lair, they never fail to throw out the one gotcha: Prove to me God exists as if they and everything around them appeared through some mystical slight-of-hand. They insist on placing the burden of persuasion on the faithful to prove God exists. I have never felt the need to be polemic about God. I have faith, and faith is the beacon that guides my life.

Logically speaking, I see life as a Venn diagram with God at the center of the intersecting universe, segments, and overlapping circles. Regardless of the number or types of circles I create, God remains firmly placed in the center. Conversely, I see the atheist and agnostic's life more like an Euler diagram where certain circles, but not all, intersect and where items not meriting inclusion —namely God—are omitted entirely from the diagram.

I wonder why atheists are so persistent in their lack of beliefs. I mean, what is the worst thing that can happen if I believe in God and the afterlife, and I am wrong? On the other hand, what if they are wrong? My faith is not a matter of hedging my bets, but I do think the downside of my beliefs is inconsequential.

I also realize through my biblical studies and many other topical books about our creator that Satan loves nothing more than for us to ignore the very words of God and adhere to man's words. The trouble is man's word and manmade laws are often the work of Satan.

In Genesis, for example, God tells us explicitly how the earth was created. It was on the first day He created light. He tells us this so if we believe in God and the Bible, we must accept that God himself is the light of the world, because God did not create the sun and moon until the fourth day. The sun was the greater light to control the day, and the moon was the lesser *light* to control the night.

God did not say He would create a satellite made of sand around Earth that would somehow reflect sunlight onto the earth. Try shining a flashlight onto a sand dune and see if the light reflects. It doesn't. The moon casts a light onto the earth. How do I know?

First, because God says so and second, it is commonsense. We have all seen the shadows created by the moon. In 1 Timothy 6:20, God warns us all when He says, *O Timothy, keep that which is committed to thy trust, avoiding profane and vain babblings, and oppositions of science falsely so called.*

So-called scientists want us to believe the moon is 280,000 miles away from earth and that the sun is nearly 93,000,000 miles from the earth. The notion that our complex world was just some strange phenomenon created by the *big bang* is ludicrous. As hard as it may be to set aside your own cognitive dissonance, the heliocentric model of earth spinning at 1,000 miles an hour at the equator through infinite space around a sun that itself is traveling at 450,000 miles per hour within a galaxy that itself is traveling at 1.3 million miles per hour is preposterous.

The more we are convinced to think of ourselves as some insignificant little planet hurdling through infinite space, the easier it is for us to wonder where Heaven is and if it really exists. If we think of ourselves as the descendants of primates, we ignore God's law. It is just that simple.

I readily admit I struggled with these concepts. After all, I too am the product of public-school programming, but in the end, I applied the common-sense God gave me along with some critical thinking and the word of God himself, and it was not long before I realized I could not reconcile what I was taught with the Word of God.

By now I suspect some of you are thinking I need to increase my dosage of my medication, but if you simply apply logic to what I have written and actually do more research, you will see the plan for the handlers of the world—the true power brokers or the globalists, if you prefer—is to methodically remove God from our lives and our lexicons. I will not do that even if it subjects me to some ridicule. Jesus was mocked, arrested, convicted, and crucified for us. It seems only fitting that I take a little heat for daring to think for myself and not blindly accepting what we have been told to believe.

If you have ever questioned the official government narratives surrounding September 11, 2001, JFK's assassination, the origin of COVID-19, Pope John Paul I's death, the suicide of Jeffrey Epstein, the unexplained death of Nicola Tesla, and recent election results, then ask yourself if you are still willing to believe everything the government tells you. Or would you rather trust your own instincts, your own independent fact finding, commonsense and, most important, the Word of God? For me, the choice is simple.

Throughout the course of my journey, I made a slight distinction between faith and trust. Some might argue those terms are completely synonymous or that one is subsumed by the other, but the distinction I draw is this: *faith* is the overarching concept that God exists and that He has our best interests in mind. *Trust* is a recognition that God is in charge and has a plan for us, whether we see it. I believe one can have faith in God but still try to control his own destiny.

Conceptually, trust requires us to give the helm to God and let Him guide our lives the way He sees fit, recognizing that course corrections are His plan, not ours. Our job, to a large extent, is to sit back and enjoy the ride and to recognize when God is telling us something we need to listen to.

Applying trust is difficult because instinctively humans desire to be in control, but sometimes we have no choice. Life is bigger than we are and when we make the decision to hand over the helm or the reins to God, He will steer us in the direction He decides we should go. Allowing God to drive can be scary, but the most amazing thing is once you reach whatever destination God has in store for you and you look around, your natural response will only be *wow*!

Whether you have faith or trust is a choice you make. I am only telling my story and, for me, faith and trust are the crucial things that helped me to recover. Mine is not a one-size-fits-all approach to recovery. If you choose to ignore this aspect of your recovery, you may. Only ask yourself who gave you the ability to make that choice. Okay, enough said. I am not here to be dogmatic about my faith.

I remember a client testified in court during a probation violation, hearing of his reconciliation with Christ and how his belief in the Lord helped him to understand who he was and who he wanted to be. A cynical prosecutor scoffed at that notion, citing my client's lengthy criminal history to suggest he was only using God now and that his stated beliefs were insincere.

A common joke in the criminal justice arena is that if one really wants to find God, he needs only to look in the jails and prisons. This was meant entirely tongue in cheek because sometimes hardened criminals would profess their faith only to turn around and commit additional crimes once released. But it is quite true that once a person is incarcerated, he often turns to God to help him cope with the stress of jail or prison life.

When I finally got the chance to respond to the prosecutor's argument, I calmly said to the judge, *I understand the joke that God can be found in jail. We have all said it, but when one really thinks about it, where else would we expect to find God—at a risqué pool party in Las Vegas? No, God sought those who were broken, and He healed their hearts, minds, and bodies. It is perfectly logical to find God in jails and prisons that are filled with people suffering from a plethora of maladies, from mental to physical, and even those of the heart and soul.* I believe my argument resonated with the judge and the defendant received a very favorable disposition.

I often talk to my clients about God and what He could do to turn their broken lives around. I never tried to be a one-man crusade, but told my clients what worked for me when my life seemed less than ideal. Sometimes I only needed to spend fifteen minutes talking about the legal issues pertaining to a client's legal case but chose to spend another forty-five minutes or so discussing in a non-intimidating or threatening way what prayer could do for them. I decided the non-threatening and less judgmental approach was preferable and carried more weight only because I had an experience that was a real turnoff.

During undergraduate school, I was playing ping-pong in the student union with a self-described born-again Christian who asked me in the middle of a game how my relationship was with the Lord. My response was, *We are getting along pretty well*. My opponent's response took me aback and I have never forgotten it.

He replied, *I don't think so*. I asked him how he knew that, and he replied, *I can just tell*. His snap judgment of me was so off-putting, I set the paddle down and walked away. I never want to be that guy, even here. Faith and trust are personal choices.

Long before I was triggered, I relied heavily on God to get me through my depression. I often found myself going midday to church and praying aloud to God to ask Him to restore my heart and mind. I entered through the office and then made my way into the chapel or the Nave. No one was ever there, so I was able to say my prayers aloud.

For some reason, I felt better hearing my own voice echoing in the cavernous Nave. I sometimes spent thirty minutes or more praying for God's blessing and healing powers. I realize God does things in His time, not mine, but I can recall when I walked out of the church completely healed from the anxiety I was feeling. I learned never to underestimate God's ability to heal a broken heart.

One expression I loved the most came from Judyth, who always reminded me God is perfect. I never understood and may never understand why I had to battle personal demons for so long, but I suspect the devil was running amok with me and saw a golden opportunity to take down a good man— not a perfect man as if one of those exists, but a genuinely good man.

Throughout my ordeal, I recited the mantra *God is perfect* in my head. I knew God had not taken me as far as He had and placed me in a position to affect so many broken lives, only to abandon me. Even as I wrote this book, which was a labor of love and healing for me, I felt divinely inspired. But I would like to view myself as merely a conduit—a vessel, if you prefer—to talk about God's goodness. Matthew Chapter 6, verses 9-13 states:

But when you pray, go into your room, close the door, and pray to your Father, who is unseen. Then your Father, who sees what is done in secret, will reward you. And when you pray, do not keep on babbling like pagans, for they think they will be heard because of their many words. Do not be like them, for your Father knows what you need before you ask him.

This, then, is how you should pray:

Our Father in heaven,

hallowed be your name,

your kingdom come,

your will be done,

on earth as it is in heaven.

Give us today our daily bread,

And forgive us our debts,

as we also have forgiven our debtors,

And lead us not into temptation,

but deliver us from the evil one.

For some people, counting sheep or listening to meditation music helps them to fall asleep. I found reciting this prayer—The Lord's Prayer—over and over in my head helped me to relax and usually fall asleep after six or seven recitations. I found so much power contained within these few words. I encourage you to try doing the same. You have nothing to lose and everything to gain.

CHAPTER 29

REDIRECT YOUR FOCUS

Turn away from yourself and your own problems and direct your attention toward someone else. Anyone who has ever gone through any traumatic event knows about the obsession that naturally follows. Whether one is fixated on the events or the resultant problems caused by the events, those feelings become all-consuming, and prevent one from living a full life. Personally, I found myself so focused on my own problems, I could not see what was directly in front of me.

At first glance, you might think I am contradicting my suggestion to put yourself first. By directing your attention toward someone else and, for a time, redirecting your energy is putting yourself first. By doing so, you will turn away from your problems and stop the maddening obsessions. Putting yourself first in its purest form means to do what is good for you, irrespective of what others may think.

Throughout my life, I tried to do right for everyone in my family, even if it meant extra work and sacrifice for myself. My attitude now is I have fulfilled my obligations. I have given my children a great foundation. I gave my wife everything she needs to continue her life. The focus now is on me.

I need to stop trying to make everyone else happy and stop sacrificing my own well-being for others. My number one priority is me. If I want to go somewhere or do something, then I only need to commit to it and make it happen. No longer will I consume myself with the repercussions of my decisions and actions.

If I had taken this approach as I was rearing my children, many could rightfully chide me for being selfish and egocentric. But I have set my children on the right path. I gave them the physical and emotional resources to be successful. They have a full life ahead of them.

CHAPTER 30
LIGHTEN YOUR LOAD

During my darkest days, I had no choice but to reduce my stress and that meant lightening my case load. I was not in the mental or physical shape to tackle some of the more complex litigation cases. Even simple cases seemed overwhelming and daunting.

You may recall how I helped a new attorney lighten his case load when he came to me completely stressed out. I did not have the luxury of having anyone do this for me, but I knew what needed to be done. I also had the blessing of God in my corner.

I spoke about the diminution of cases that caused me to stress, but what I failed to see at the time was God was protecting me from myself. I have often heard God will never give you more than you can handle, though I often felt as if I was teetering on the edge. In hindsight, God gave enough to sustain my law practice, but not so much as to overwhelm me.

Stress kills! In case I did not say it loudly or clearly enough, let me repeat it—STRESS KILLS! It kills in a variety of ways. Physically, it affects the operation of every major organ in your body: it raises your blood pressure, hardens your arteries, and can absolutely cause heart attacks.

Psychologically, stress is just as bad, if not worse. Stress, especially stress leading to anxiety, makes us feel out of control, as if we are going crazy. It makes us take CBD/THC gummies, smoke pot, drink to excess, take harmful controlled substances, and act out in ways too numerous to mention, but that include punching metal U-Haul ramps, the sides of your own house, and wooden tables with what seems like superhuman strength. This might be called testosterone or adrenaline overload, and when that energy gets so bottled up that it needs to be expelled, it will. One can only hope the energy is directed toward an inanimate object and not toward another person.

I know for a fact that jails and prisons are filled with people who acted impulsively and who directed their anger or stress at others. I have represented many of them. Often, I am asked how I can defend someone I know is guilty.

I can for a variety of reasons, but primarily because I believe many good people—because of stress, anxiety, hopelessness, despair, depression, or some other life-altering circumstances—made very poor decisions. You know, like the poor decisions I made whenever I called A to help me evict my deadbeat tenants or when I punched the metal ramp. Those were dumb decisions made by a man who, by all accounts, had his life pretty much together.

I am happy people intervened in my life at just the right time to help me lighten my load so I would not be overwhelmed to the point of no return. This is the very point. I saw myself spiraling out of control and perhaps it was because of the experience of September 11, 2001, and my brother's suicide, that I was slightly better equipped to understand what was happening. Despite my knowledge, I still felt nothing but hopelessness.

What about the people who experience these symptoms for the first time? What must they think? I was supposedly better prepared than many, having already lived through certain traumas in my life and yet I felt no more prepared than I was in 2001. I can completely see how a person would want to give up and end his life. I came close too, but in the back of my mind I could see a glimmer of hope that things would get better if I could only ride out the pain and suffering. In the back of my mind, I thought about Scott. I thought about my children and what my suicide would do to them. And in a strange sort of way, I thought of Jimmy V's verity to never ever give up.

I never made the conscious decision to lighten my load. I believe God made that decision for me and I am grateful for it. Make no mistake, we can do certain things preemptively to lighten our loads, so we hopefully never find ourselves in a bad predicament.

I cut back on the cases I used to take. No longer do I maintain the belief that I must solve everyone's problems or that I must be able to do every area of law. I am a lawyer, but I hold no divine right.

CHAPTER 31

JOURNAL

J ournaling is nothing more than writing down your thoughts and emotions at the time you are feeling them. It is a historical account you can later review to see how far you have come. I resisted it at first, thinking it was a waste of time. I was wrong.

I did not overthink or make it overly complicated. For me, journaling was a simple email I would send to myself only to chronicle the stages of my anxiety and depression. Much like a weightlifter keeps a log of his exercises to track his progress, a journal acts as a barometer of one's feelings at the time he is going through them. The real utility with journaling is to go back and see where you started and hopefully how far you have pro-gressed.

This book started out as a journal, and each of those emails morphed into a paragraph that later morphed into a chapter. Below are three of my redacted email journals:

~

From: rwegman

Sent: Wednesday, July 13, 2022 1:43 PM

To: rwegman

Subject: Journal

Today i had a bond hearing for a guy charged with attempted rape. I was unsure what was required for attempted rape of a minor. That made me anx-ious. I can't tell if people can sense my anxiety and that makes me even more anxious. I feel like it's obvious.

Last night i felt great and even this morning but after the bond hearing I took a pill. I then did some research so I'm better prepared for the appeal.

XXXXXXXX Scott came in at noon to discuss XXXX's case. I felt okay, but I'm just wondering what it would take to get him to plead. I don't know how I'm going to come up with a defense for this guy. That makes me anxious.

Sometimes I feel like the weight of the world is on my shoulders.

I just know what I'm going to do to regain my confidence and stop this crazy anxiety. I'm so sick of it.

I canceled my reservation for the steakhouse because i just want some time to myself. I hope I feel up to going to the gym. I'm definitely tired and maybe the lack of sleep is making my situation worse. I woke up at 0600.

Sent from my iPhone

From: rwegman

Sent: Wednesday, June 29, 2022 3:23 PM

To: rwegman

Subject: Journal

I tried to get away from the office because it was slow and I didn't see the point of sitting around. Plus, I was feeling anxious. Not sure why.

I pulled into my driveway and got a text from XXX about a new client who was scheduled when I had to drive to Cape Charles. I rescheduled it for Friday at 10.

Looks like the bond appeal will not be on the docket. I now have to note the appeal and then set it. Not sure why doing all this basic shit is making me anxious, but it is. It's so frustrating to feel anxious for no valid reason. I really wish someone could handle all my shit for me so I could catch a break. I feel like I'm responsible for the world sometimes and I'm one person.

I'm sitting outside in the lounge chair, trying to relax. It's so hard. It's also strange that once it's 5 pm, my anxiety level goes way down. I guess it's because, at that point, I'm more in control.

Sent from my iPhone

From: rwegman Sent: Friday, June 24, 2022 9:02 PM

To: rwegman

Subject: Journal

I went to the gym 3 times. I lifted weights and rode the bike. The 1st time I went into the sauna, I could not feel the heat. My skin felt cold so I got out.

I went back again and rode the bike. I felt good. Between the 2nd and the 3rd, I went to Jason's Deli and had a muffuletta and a salad. The 3rd time I lifted a little, and I rode the bike and the stair climber 10 floors.

I was on the phone with XXXXXXXXX for a little while. I spoke with XXXXX too. Everything seemed much better.

I really thought I had a nervous breakdown and I still feel like I did, but after a while the pressure subsided and I could think clearly. I also spoke with XXXXXXXXX about the Walmart case.

Finally, I took Oscar for a walk. He is exhausted, but he really enjoyed running on the golf course. It's 9 pm and I'm sitting on the deck relaxing. I'm excited but a little anxious to see XXXXXXX if she comes Sunday. I'm going to go to the gym after she leaves to try to stave off any setback.

One other thing. I trimmed the bushes in the back and one or 2 in the front. I need to throw away the branches, but it's a start.

I tried to get Wi-Fi working on the TV, but for some reason the internet is not connected. I wanted to watch a show for the first time in a long time. I feel like a little TV would be a good distraction for me. All my music seems sad now. It's beautiful but sad.

I just hope I can keep this up for the rest of the weekend. It feels pretty normal. I love it.

Sent from my iPhone

CHAPTER 32
LAUGH - CRY -THINK

In the Introduction, I discussed Coach V's philosophy about life. Near the end of this speech, he recommended people do three things: laugh, cry, and think. He said if you really think about it, if you can spend every day doing just those three things, you will have had one hell of a day.

~

LAUGH

Whether we are hanging out with friends and family or watching a comedy show, we often find ourselves laughing. Laughing never fails to make you feel good. It does not matter what makes you laugh. Whenever you laugh, certain healthy chemicals are released.

Even during my darkest moments, I tried to find the humor in life. I have always had the kind of personality that brought out laughter in others, but the greatest and funniest times were when I laughed at myself. I still believe self-deprecating humor is best. It is not only funny, but it also says you are not taking yourself too seriously.

The expression laughter is the best medicine is quite accurate. Laughter has several great health benefits, among them being a boost to our immune systems to lowering our blood pressure and clearing the mind. Many medical articles suggest laughter activates T cells, the cells that help one's body stay healthy.

I also learned that the heart is profoundly affected by laughter. Though exercise and healthy foods are important for your heart health, according to the Cleveland Clinic, laughing increases blood flow to your heart like the way aerobic exercise increases your blood flow. The surge of extra blood to your heart can help reduce many heart-related issues.

∿

CRY

If I had collected my tears over the past year into a bucket, it would have absolutely overflowed. I know men and boys are encouraged not to cry. Crying is considered unmanly and weak, but nothing could be further from the truth. I know not how that started, but that very philosophy has likely hurt more boys and men than anything else. At times, I felt if I did not cry, I would have exploded. I used to withhold tears, but crying is simply in my nature, and I am not ashamed of it.

We cried when we were babies, but as soon as we became adults, crying was suddenly taboo. Many, especially boys, try to keep themselves from crying based on some fallacy that crying is a sign of weakness. But crying is quite healthy. Science claims that crying releases stress and is one of the keys to staying mentally healthy. They further claim emotional tears contain high levels of stress hormones. Emotional tears also contain more mood-regulating manganese than other types of tears. Stress tightens muscles and heightens tension, so when you cry you release some of that. Crying activates the parasympathetic nervous system and restores the body to a state of balance.

I never really thought about the health benefits of crying or why I always felt better after crying. I cried over the loss of my wife. I cried because I earnestly believed I would spend my entire life alone and without love. I cried when I was alone.

I cried about the breakup of my family. I cried when I went to the church to pray and to see my priest, and I cried about Judyth and our breakup. In short, I cried about everything, but the thing I noticed was just after a good cry, my mood changed drastically. I always felt better.

The one place I never really cried was in my therapist's office. I do not know why and maybe it is perhaps because we never really got into the things that took me to that point. I was rather focused on the things that would improve my quality of life and my outlook on life.

THINK

Perhaps it seems basic. We are all living, breathing, thinking creatures whose brains seemingly turn into mush unless we do something to stimulate them. At various times in my life, I have read books, done crossword puzzles, learned foreign languages. Honestly, my job alone is cerebral, but if one does not think about something positive, his mind will often gravitate to the worst possible unhealthy option. That was part of my problem. I let my mind control me instead of the other way around.

My mind was a purveyor of doom and gloom. One thing that helped me tremendously was learning Spanish. I got onto the Duolingo App and studied anytime I had a free moment. If I was focused on something like Spanish, I could not possibly let my mind drift into uncharted areas filled with uncertainty and perceived perils.

One of my best days was when I was trying to find the proverbial needle in a haystack of legal research. For some crazy reason, my mind was hitting on all cylinders this day and I felt like my old self. Even writing this book has required me to go back and think about syntax, word choices, and sentence structure. Anytime I could be formulating my next sentence or paragraph was a period of time I could not dwell on the negative thoughts that so often consumed me.

The mind is extremely powerful, but if we allow it to control us, we are doomed. We must find a way to control and tame it. I am still no master at this and so I will have good days and bad days and, oddly enough, I have little control over which will be the order of the day. But I do know that keeping the mind occupied (i.e., thinking) has helped me tremendously in overcoming the fears and anxiety that occur when one feels like his mind is spinning free like a roulette wheel, never knowing where the little ball is going to land.

CHAPTER 33

LIVE IN THE PRESENT MOMENT

This was the most difficult concept of all the ones I learned and yet I preached this to clients almost daily. I felt the need to map out my entire life and, in one sense, my life had already been mapped out. I had two children —a boy and a girl. I had the house sans a white picket fence, but I had a beach house. Most important, I had a wife with whom I would grow old.

Suddenly, my plan was destroyed. I either had to create a new plan for myself or as Ben Stiller said to Jennifer Aniston in *Along Came Polly*, I had to commit to being on the non-plan plan. Said another way, I had to live each day as if the day was a mini plan. Said a third and more clinical way, I had to live each day in the present moment.

Living in the present moment simply means avoiding thinking too far ahead in your life, but enjoying the minute, hour, or day you are presently experiencing. Most of us look forward to our weekends and dread Mondays, especially if we have a big presentation or other work-related issue set for Monday or the following week. If we pull away from work on Fridays and allow our minds to think about the coming Monday, we will never enjoy Saturday and Sunday and what have we really accomplished?

Dwelling on the beginning of the next work week will not make it arrive any sooner or delay it any further. Monday will come when Monday is supposed to come, and thinking about before it arrives is an exercise in futility. We only get ourselves worked up about things we have no control over. As difficult as it is to avoid these thoughts, you must find a way to distract yourself to get your mind back on track. For me, music, journaling, or just riding around in my car were all distractions that worked for me.

Of course, if you really have a big presentation or case that is set for the following week and you are not prepared to do it, no matter how hard you try, you will probably not live in the present moment.

If that is the case, your best option might be to go into the office or wherever to ensure you are prepared.

After you feel prepared, you will probably have a much easier time shoving that issue on the back burner or into the farthest recesses of your mind. You can see how none of these suggestions is mutually exclusive but interrelated.

CHAPTER 34

ORGANIZE

I already stated I am no expert on anxiety, but one thing I learned to alleviate the symptoms of anxiety is to be more organized. As a predominantly right brain thinker, I was never good at planning or organizing. People often asked whether I would like to be a prosecutor. I have prosecuted cases both as a military lawyer and as a Special Assistant United States Attorney. But to prosecute requires one to think about the witnesses one might need to prove the elements of every criminal charge and then to subpoena them well before the start of the case.

I could do it, but it was difficult for me. I simply was not the type of person to think ahead. I was one of those people whose office looked like a tornado touched down and scattered everything into a giant mess. But I had a system that worked for me. I would use the oft-cited phrase *there is a method to my madness.*

But once my self-esteem took a hit and anxiety ensued, my disorganization created a huge problem for me. Anytime I had to hunt down my watch, a pen, my wallet, or anything else, including the very clothing ensemble I would wear to court created anxiety. I found that planning what clothes I would wear, ensuring they were clean and pressed, and laying them out in advance tremendously reduced my anxiety.

I still give myself a pat down while calling out the items I need. I will say wallet—check; pens—check; keys—check and so on until I am sure I have everything I might need. This little pat down method ensures I have everything I need for court or for just about any activity that may require some level of planning and preparation.

During the peak of my anxiety and depression, I took nothing for granted. I did all my research well in advance and wrote down as many bullet points as needed to ensure that I would have a back-up plan just in case I froze. I am happy to say, however, that I never froze.

I never gave much thought to doing my criminal cases. I had done so many cases in the past I could practically do them in my sleep. It was not uncommon for me to open a file and completely conduct the trial from just my memory, occasionally looking down only to remember my client's name. But desperate times called for desperate measures and I wasn't taking any chances with myself or with the people who counted on me.

CHAPTER 35
HYGIENE AND BODY IMAGE

This seems basic, but when one is in the throes of deep, dark depression or anxiety, hygiene can be easily overlooked. Anxiety and depression can sometimes be easy to spot just from one's physical appearance.

At times, I looked at myself and thought my appearance was a little disheveled. My hair was longer than I usually liked it and I had many more gray hairs on my head and longer facial hairs than I usually kept. Consequently, I failed to feel good about myself. Recognizing this as an important factor, I did not go too long before getting a haircut, getting my clothes laundered and pressed, and trimming my facial hair.

Appearance is extremely important to one's self esteem. Looking your best is important because not only do people make snap judgments about you, especially if they are used to seeing you more put together, but it also makes you feel better about yourself.

I am not sure whether the Diagnostic and Statistical Manual of Mental Disorders (DSM), the so-called bible of psychological disorders, might call this condition, but I believe I might suffer from the opposite of anorexia nervosa.

Anorexia, as it is called, is the condition where someone of normal stature sees herself as being fat and consequently refuses to eat. The most famous person in my lifetime who suffered and ultimately died of this disorder was Karen Carpenter. Karen made up half of the duet known as the Carpenters, with the other half being her brother Richard. If silk made a sound, I believe it would sound like the voice of Karen Carpenter.

My condition knows no name and doesn't seem to be fatal, but it is the exact opposite of anorexia. Instead of being of a normal stature but seeing a fat person, I saw a runt—a 95-pound weakling. You may not believe this, but as a young boy, I actually peeled potatoes and ate them raw, thinking that the starch would fatten me up. Oh, what I wouldn't give to have that problem now.

Unfortunately, I now see my weight as it is. I no longer see myself as skinny but as pleasingly plump. I was picked on and disrespected my entire adolescent life because I was so skinny. In college, I was dating a German exchange student who just happened to be one of the prettiest girls in the entire school. How I got her or what she saw in me is as mysterious as the whereabouts of Jimmy Hoffa, who literally disappeared overnight.

Anyway, I was coming out of the cafeteria line with my girlfriend when a group of baseball jocks began audibly ogling over her. This made me so angry that I walked over to their table, slammed my tray down, and told them I did not appreciate their comments that were disrespectful to me and her. Half the guys at the table laughed, knowing there was nothing I could do about it, and the other half quieted down. But all that mattered to me at that moment was I protected my girlfriend's honor and my own.

CHAPTER 36

SOOTHE YOUR SENSES

Music has been and always will be my great passion. Growing up as a young boy, I was exposed to various genres of music as a courtesy of my parents. I learned to love and appreciate everything from classical music and the bolero to Elvis and, of course, my mom's all-time favorite, Tom Jones. But the music that inspired me the most always had some sort of catchy beat and I found myself involuntarily and rhythmically tapping to each tune played on my parent's German Grundig record player or their reel-to-reel audiotape player.

In seventh grade, I signed up for band class. That enhanced my love for and knowledge of music. For the first time, I understood time signatures, rhythmic patterns, tonality, tempos, and the instruments for which those things were so important. To this day, I can listen to music and be mesmerized by one simple drum stroke, an asymmetrical rhythm, or a dissonant chord I think is brilliantly placed. Sometimes, it is just the different timbre inserted strategically into a musical composition that turns an ordinary piece into the extraordinary.

Soon after joining the band, I realized I had something special. Music just seemed to come naturally to me, and I was soon asked not only to play at other middle schools but also the high school that was not blessed with talented percussionists.

I was successful at music and played many gigs at restaurants. One of my all-time favorite gigs was at a place called the Country Squire in Warsaw, North Carolina. This place exemplified fine dining to me.

The man who arranged the ensembles was a well-known regional piano player and vocalist by the name of Sid Willoughby. Depending on whether Sid was arranging a trio, quartet or larger, Sid called the drummer (often me), the wind and horn players, and the guitar players. Musicians never rehearsed together. Someone, usually Sid, just called out a melody and a key signature and away we went.

One gig I will never forget involved a guy who brought in several guitars, including an impressive double-neck guitar. He had all the high-end equipment, for sure. The trouble was he only knew a few musical compositions and only knew bits and pieces of those, and we were expected to fill up four sets of fifty minutes with ten-minute breaks in between. We started out strong and then ended with a sputter while people continued to dine.

During a break we tried to come up with something we could piece together in its entirety. Maybe we came up with a few, I cannot even recall, but it was decided I would do an extended drum solo to fill up some time.

I improvised on my drum kit for as long as I could while getting strange looks from the crowd like what in the hell is going on here? I can only imagine couples going home that evening thinking nothing could have been more romantic than dining by candlelight while listening to an extended improvised drum solo. Those were fun days and the stories of playing percussion could fill its own book, but the takeaway for me is that music is a source of relaxation and reflection.

In the early days of my separation, I felt tremendous burning anxiety, but once I powered up the digital synthesizer, my anxiety immediately ceased as if by magic. I never watched television, I only listened to music. My song selections were not always healthy, like when I was addicted to Adele, whose complete album was filled with sorrowful songs about her own divorce. But her songs were still melodic and enchanting, and they resonated with me.

My musical tastes varied from day to day. Some days I would listen only to jazz. On other days I listened to classical music, and still other days I listened to country music. My playlist is about as eclectic as one can be. Lately, I have been listening to Latin music.

The passion, rhythms, and lyrics are unmatched in any other genre, as far as I can tell. Apparently, my Bose noise-cancelling headphones are great at keeping ambient noises from penetrating my ears, but do a rather poor job at containing the sound within them. On more than one occasion while sitting in the dry hot sauna, I have had other people comment on my interesting playlist.

I had always watched musical talent shows like American Idol and The Voice and was always intrigued by the judge's comments. They often told contestants singing was storytelling and that they needed to feel the song and not only recite the words. Conceptually, I understood the comment, but until I went through my emotional struggle, I did not really hear the difference. I always focused on voice quality and pitch rather than on the message.

What I found so fascinating was songs I heard a thousand times before suddenly resonated with me and, for the first time, I began to hear the pain contained within the lyrics. We have probably all heard Frank Sinatra's rendition of *My Way*. It was catchy, melodic, classy, and unmistakably Sinatra, or so I thought.

I later learned the song was written by a Mexican composer and first sung in Spanish. It is called *A Mi Minera*. I might have understood why I did not comprehend the lyrics in Spanish, but I had heard a derivative of the song (not a verbatim translation) in English too many times to count and yet until I went through my struggle, I never understood them. I began looking at *A Mi Minera* (*My Way*) as my personal anthem. One thing is certain: I absolutely did things my way.

Anytime I liked a song, I would repeat it over and over until I grew tired of it. Although I had heard

My Way probably a thousand times before, I must have played it another thousand because, to me, the song took on a whole new meaning.

William Congreve, an English author of the late seventeenth and early eighteenth centuries, first stated in his play *The Mourning Bride* that music has charms to soothe a savage beast. Nothing could be truer. Anytime I felt sad, angry, heartbroken, or bitter, I played music. During my time in exile, I never watched television and relied on music to either brighten my spirits or to bring me to such an emotional state that crying was inevitable.

If I am driving my car, my music will always play, usually at an ear-piercing volume, but music was my first love, and it remains an integral part of my life. Shortly after my separation, my car needed a new alternator. The mechanics needed to replace my battery as well.

The trouble with cars today is they are so computerized, none of the electrical niceties work, including the radio, without a reset code. That code needed to come from the dealership, but I did not have the patience or the mental wherewithal to schedule the appointment.

Prior to losing access to my radio, I was an avid listener of the Bobby Bones syndicated country radio show. My morning was never complete unless I had my bacon, egg, and cheese bagel, vanilla hazelnut coffee, and a few minutes of the Bobby Bones show.

Something about Bobby's show made my day. I think it is a combination of his genuine kindness and dry wit. I have truly never heard Bobby say a harsh word about anyone. When the world was preoccupied with news about Covid cases and deaths in particular, Bobby and his studio cast always delivered a little levity on my short ride to the courthouse or to the office.

I grew particularly fond of what he calls the positivity segment, *Tell Me Something Good*. This was the part of the show where a studio member shared a story about something good or inspirational. It could be about a kitten rescued from a fire or someone doing a special deed for a person or family in need. Whatever the story, it was always a departure from the barrage of negative news stories that clogged the airwaves and permeated my subconscious.

In between those segments, Bobby played just enough country music to satisfy country purists. I enjoyed the repartee between the guests and the cast much more than the music. I knew I enjoyed this part of my morning, but I never appreciated how much I would miss it until I had to do without.

I never got my car repaired. I had every intention of doing it, but once I arrived at the dealership, I was bitten by the new car bug. The new car for me was a two-year-old car with low mileage, a few more creature comforts and, most important, a working radio.

The funny part of this purchase was that in her attempt to help me get my life together, Judyth said I should buy new floor mats. I went back to the dealership to buy the floor mats but came away with a new car instead. When I announced this to Judyth, she said little.

Later I learned her daughter thought I may have gotten things mixed up because of the slight language barrier. Her daughter thought maybe I had misinterpreted buying floor mats for my old car with buying a new car. I think Judyth felt bad until I explained I perfectly understood her broken English.

CHAPTER 37
THINK OF THUMPER

MY mother always told us growing up to *remember what Thumper said.* I had no idea who Thumper was, but she told us this repeatedly. Thumper, it turns out, is the little bunny rabbit in the Disney classic, Bambi, who commented unkindly about how unsteady Bambi was on his feet. Thumper's comment about Bambi prompted Thumper's mother to ask him what his father told him.

Thumper replied, *If you can't say something nice, don't say nothing at all.* Despite knowing nothing about Thumper, I still always considered that solid advice, and I tried to incorporate it into my daily life. A corollary might also be, *If you have something nice to say, say it.*

I thought long and hard about how I wanted to end this book and I concluded this was the perfect place to discuss how we can make this world better for us, our children, and our children's children. I decided the advice Thumper's mother gave to Thumper is a good place to start. As simple as that is, for reasons I cannot explain, the advice seems so difficult for many to follow. Again, I am guilty too.

Biblically speaking, I will not be so brazen as to cast the first stone. The Bible also commands us to love one another as we love ourselves and to do unto others as we would do unto ourselves. The latter, the so-called Golden Rule, appears to be so basic and yet it seems to be difficult for many to follow. I have heard people jokingly say do unto others before they do unto you. That is both funny and sad, but it is understandable.

Some people can be ruthless and cunning. But the presumption should be that most people are good. I have gotten burned a few times thinking this way (ala Don), but I would rather treat people with dignity and respect and take my lumps now and then than indict all people and feel like the world is filled with sinister people.

I try my best to be kind to people from all walks of life, whether it is a janitor cleaning the restrooms, a receptionist, a cashier, or a person taking my order at the drive through. Kindness is free and if you attempt to be kind and it is not reciprocated, do not fret and say, how dare that #@%*&#%$? Kindness comes from your heart. It is something you do instinctively because the spirit moves you, not because you expect to get something in return.

You also do not know what may be on that person's mind. Maybe they or a loved one were recently diagnosed with cancer. Maybe their spouse just left or passed away. Maybe their child is being bullied in school, is addicted to drugs, or is incarcerated. You get the point and that is, we just do not know and for that reason, the default should be to treat others with dignity and respect.

Since going through my own difficulties, I have become more in tune and empathetic to the plights of others. When a car tries to squeeze in front of me while I have been waiting in line, rather than reacting by honking and extending my middle finger I think to myself: *Maybe they just got word that their loved one is in the hospital, and they are rushing to see them. Or maybe they are being a jerk,* but the point is we don't know. My attitude now is to flash my lights, slow down, and wave to the person. I still arrive at my destination in a timely manner, and I am just as happy. You may have set an example for the person and maybe next time they will do the same thing for another driver.

The concept of paying it forward has been around for a long time. I have heard of people in a drive-through line paying the tab for the person to follow or the person in a checkout line paying for the groceries of another. Every time I hear of it, I find that the person who was surprised and treated by another often pays it forward until the chain is eventually broken.

An act of kindness does not have to involve money. A simple greeting, a witty joke, or a kind word can be all it takes to brighten someone's day. When I was in Indy with my son for DCI finals, the lines at the concession stands were atrocious. But instead of getting frustrated and taking it out on the people serving the food as fast as they could, many thanked them for working so hard. I also acknowledged their hard work verbally and with a smile.

One of the cashiers filling orders was trying to get someone's attention. Apparently, he knew this man. He held out his fist to give the guy a fist bump, but the man failed to see him. I saw the cashier with his fist extended and told him I would not leave him hanging. I fist bumped the man and thought no more about it.

A few minutes later, the man returned to me and said thank you. He said that was the nicest thing that happened to him all day and that I made his day. When I gave that man a fist bump, it was really to be funny. Little did I realize the impact that simple gesture would have on the man who had worked all day and night, filling orders for the massive crowd. I still do not know what the cashier may have been going through, but apparently a fist bump was all it took to brighten his day.

Recently at the drive-through at a local pharmacy, I stopped to inquire about one of my anxiety medications. I had not run out but was running low. Perhaps the pharmacist recognized two things: they were late filling the prescription and not having the medication would increase my anxiety. Without uttering a word, she left her position at the drive-through and filled it on the spot.

I can only say, historically, this never happens. I was always told to check back the following day or to expect a text message in several hours. But this very kind woman filled my prescription while I waited. I told her this was unprecedented, and I profusely thanked her. She beamed from ear to ear and told me I was very welcome.

Truthfully, she gained nothing tangible by going out of her way for me, but what she got in return was a sincere thank you and recognition that what she did was extremely kind. This is another example of how a simple act by her and a simple acknowledgment of thanks by me was all that was needed to make each other's day.

If we only were a little more generous with our *pleases* and *thank you's*; if we occasionally paid it forward; if we offered a few more fist bumps; and if we were to only think about Thumper, what a wonderful world we would have. The first hundred years may in fact be the hardest, but we can each make them a little less hard by caring for our fellowmen and women in ways that are so simple and yet so impactful.

CHAPTER 38
HUMILITY & SELF WORTH

When you find someone you love and who loves you back, fight like hell every day to hold on to it. Like a potted plant, that relationship must be fortified to grow. True love is precious and it may only come along once in a lifetime. Contrary to a well-known maxim, the grass is not always greener on the other side.

I have heard it said women have to kiss a lot of frogs to find their prince. I think men must do the same to find their princess. If sex is all you are after, that is a choice you make, but if love and commitment are what you seek, you may find them to be far more elusive.

In my humble opinion, we should never be in search of a prince or princess. Those are fairytale aspirations. Rather, we should seek an ordinary partner who has the capacity for requited love and who will make himself or herself emotionally available during good and bad times. Trust that regardless of one's socioeconomic status or station in life, bad times will happen. They are inevitable.

Whenever my wife reminded me of how I failed to treat her like the princess her father told her she should be, I first thought, *I am not a prince and never learned princely etiquette.* Second, I understood that the life of a princess is not always what it is cracked up to be.

I can only think of the late Princess Diana Frances Spencer, Princess of Wales; Her Royal Highness, Sarah Ferguson, the Duchess of York, and Princess Meghan Markle as recent examples. Their lives were certainly not fairytales. Even the late Grace Kelly, who became the Serene Highness Grace of Monaco, died tragically when she lost control of her car that careened down a mountainside in that tiny country.

Roughly a century before Princess Diana et al., in 1899, Maurice Ravel wrote his now famous musical composition entitled *Pavane pour une infante dé-*

funte, literally translated from French to English to mean Pavane for a dead princess. This morose yet hauntingly beautiful composition only foreshadowed what was to befall the monarchies in England and the tiny country of Monaco.

The point is, we are all ordinary people with what are ordinary dreams and desires and the moment we lose sight of those and place ourselves, or allow ourselves to be placed, on a pedestal, we become vulnerable. For as much as America welcomes success and fulfillment of the American dream, many Americans also love to see someone get his bell rung occasionally.

Recall I discussed my BMW 528i and how someone was destined to see me pay for my success. After all, who was I to be driving around in a car that exemplified status? Make no mistake, people should have the choice and the luxury to enjoy the fruits of their labor and sacrifice. But I drove that car mostly because it was fast, beautiful, luxurious, and it made me feel good, not because I needed to impress anyone else.

A local restaurant offered only valet service and the valets always parked the more expensive cars in the front row where they were backed in for anyone walking by to see. Perhaps it was to protect the cars, or perhaps it was only to enjoy watching the people gawk at the cars. My sense was that in the owner's eyes, those cars elevated the restaurant to a higher status.

I would be lying if I said I did not enjoy seeing my car parked among the other luxury cars, but when I got rid of that car, I never looked back. At this point in my life, I do not care if I am parked in the front row or the last row if I am somewhere in the row.

Scripture teaches us to be humble, and humility is one of the most important keys to life. One can be a good person, be charitable, do all or most of the right things and still be the target of character assassination if he adopts an attitude of self-importance.

When I was in the Coast Guard and standing watch as duty officer, I was the man in charge. Once, during the grounding of an oil tanker in New York Harbor, I had been up all night ensuring an adequate federal response to a potential oil spill. I had run the show and was exhausted by morning. The Captain of the Port of New York directed me to brief the Commander of Vessel Traffic Service (VTS) about the incident. I promptly did so.

I believe the VTS Commander took one look at my rank and thought, how could this young man possibly tell him anything that he did not already know? He was flippant, dismissive, and frankly rude.

I just looked at him and literally said, *fine*. I was the Group Duty Officer who ran the operation, but if he did not want to be briefed about what transpired, I would go to bed. His tone abruptly changed, and he asked me to bring him up to speed on the response operation.

He outranked me by two ranks. I was a lieutenant, and he was a commander, but in that moment, rank was irrelevant. I knew something he did not and yet his arrogance and preconceived notions about me based only on my subordinate rank led him to believe I could not possibly teach him anything. In short, his lack of humility almost interfered with the exchange of information useful to him, but privy only to me.

The military is filled with Type-A personalities, so it is not surprising at all that many senior officers can be pretentious and condescending. When I lived on the Coast Guard base on Governors Island, New York, I was fortunate to get housing typically reserved for the upper echelon of the officer corp. My apartment overlooked the Statue of Liberty, but I was a junior officer—a Lieutenant Junior Grade—when I first moved there.

One guy who lived in the apartment above mine seemed to look down his nose at my family and me. I feel certain he wondered how I was able to live in housing reserved for the crème de la crème of the junior officer corp. If I were to make up a phrase that best described his attitude toward people holding inferior rank, I would say he characterized us as the scum de la scum.

I used to say hello whenever I saw him, and he never responded. I finally gave up and decided he would get no more *good morning* or *hello* from me. Then one Christmas morning, I stepped out of my apartment and saw him. Feeling jubilant about the holiday, I broke my protocol and wished him a Merry Christmas. His response is one I will never forget. He turned away from me and said, *indeed*. I can laugh about that now, but at the time I found his comment insulting.

I saw a pathetic little man with an ego and sense of self-worth that far exceeded his stature. My father, a retired enlisted man himself, would often say when an enlisted man salutes an officer, the enlisted man is really saying he is a worthless piece of garbage.

When the officer salutes back, he is acknowledging that the enlisted man is a worthless piece of garbage. That sentiment is an extremely cynical way of looking at this time-honored custom and courtesy, but it made me wonder what my neighbor thought about those in the enlisted ranks if he found it disdainful speaking to a man of only one rank subordinate to his.

The point of all this and this entire book is to say, as a child of God, you are important no matter what others think, say, or do to convince you otherwise. Let their own lack of humility or self-worth not affect how you feel about yourself. Anxiety often stems from fear—fear of public speaking, rejection, or the unknown; fear of heights and just about anything you can conjure up. But if we believe in ourselves and do not allow ourselves to be ripped apart by others or by the unpredictable circumstances of life, we can at least control fear.

Fear is a perfectly natural emotion that helps us survive. Without it, we would not know when it is time to scream and run when Jason from *Friday the 13th* is on our heels. But an unhealthy fear is one not justified by the objective facts. This type of fear leads to massive anxiety as one's fight-or-flight response goes into hyperdrive.

Anxiety can also be caused by trauma—trauma of domestic abuse, war, divorce, the death or terminal diagnosis of a loved one, to name a few. We may not have as much control over the traumas that can suddenly strike, but we can hopefully understand that when our bodies (most notably our minds) relive those traumas, we have the means to shut off that valve using the same mind that reacted to the trauma.

Kelli used to tell me, whenever I felt my mind careening out of control—or whenever I heard that familiar and extremely annoying buzzing or humming associated with anxiety particularly in my left ear—I should acknowledge it, wave it off, and divert my attention away from it. Those three steps rarely work for me, but at least they were affirmative steps I could take to divert my attention away from the source.

I also know my feelings are shared by millions of others. I find some solace in knowing my condition is not unique.

CHAPTER 39
THE FINAL ANALYSIS

Time really does heal all. The key to success is to take the time you need to focus on yourself. I have heard it said to never make a permanent decision about a temporary situation. That is a good reminder that we should not make hasty decisions based on temporary circumstances. Just say to yourself *this too shall pass*. As difficult as times were for me, I fought like hell to survive, and you can too.

I hope if this book does anything, it lets you know a few things: you are not crazy, you are not alone, and you will overcome even the worst part of the storm you are going through. Everyone tells you your life will improve; it only takes time. I cannot say how long it will take for you to finally be free from the mental shackles that bind you or to realize your true potential.

Your recovery may steer you in a completely different direction. Either way, choose a pathway that works for you and if you come to a roadblock, knock it down. Or, as Yogi Berra said, *if you come to a fork in the road, take it.* But keep pushing forward as if your life depends on it because it does.

Recently, my wife was diagnosed with diabetes and then she was told she had pancreatic cancer. I nearly dropped to my knees when I heard the news. I understood the survival rate for pancreatic cancer, even in the best circumstance and with the best medical treatment, is roughly five years. I found myself uncontrollably sobbing over the prospect of losing her.

Her unfortunate diagnosis forced me to rethink everything. For as much as I voraciously fought with my wife and seethed at times for her leaving me and causing me to incur the mental and physical shock waves I described throughout this book, I realize she is the woman I loved for nearly all my adult life. She will always be the mother of my children. I do not want to attend my son and daughter's wedding as the only surviving parent.

This sudden and strange turn of events regarding her medical condition forced me to come to terms with our relationship and with my responses to our divorce. I once resented giving her anything, even though I knew it was right to do. But now I am willing to give her everything she needs if she can find the best medical doctor at the best hospital. I do not want to lose her. I do not want her to think about how she will pay her bills while she is recovering from surgery.

I am not speaking as a martyr or as someone who seeks credit for his benevolence. I am speaking as a man who once shared a wonderful life with a woman I do not want to see die or be shackled by living expenses.

Suddenly, the spousal support seems like a small price to pay to keep her in my life. Just as paying for my children's cell phone bill and student loans makes me feel more *fatherly* and needed, paying my wife's spousal support makes me feel like I can take at least one burden off of her shoulders. What I used to resent and detest, I now pay with glee.

I put her through hell at times and now is my chance to give her whatever she needs. I am happy to say that this excruciatingly difficult and ugly chapter of our lives went the same way as her inner organs—removed and discarded, but not forgotten.

Prior to her surgery, I researched her diagnosis and spoke with a local surgeon about her condition. It turns out the only accurate way for a doctor to know if she has cancer is to do what is called a Whipple procedure, otherwise known as a pancreaticoduodenectomy.

A Whipple procedure was named after Dr. Allen Oldfather Whipple, then surgeon-in-chief at Columbia Presbyterian Hospital. Dr. Whipple was the first to do the procedure. The procedure removes the head of the pancreas, the duodenum, the gallbladder, and the bile duct.

I was especially relieved to know my wife was going to have her Whipple procedure performed at Columbia Presbyterian Hospital. My wife is now recovering from the procedure and can look forward to a long healthy life provided she pays attention to her diet and gets regularly scheduled medical checkups. Many prayed for her health and her biopsy showed minimal cancer. I cannot be happier for her, for my children, her family, and myself.

The murder case I was working on when I had my gummy attack came to a sudden and unexpected conclusion. It turned out that one of the prosecutor's witnesses was a man I had represented a few years prior, setting up an actual conflict of interest. I had no choice but to withdraw from the case to comply with my ethical obligations. I would have done great with that trial, but I had no choice.

I have even come to terms with my late father-in-law and our often-tempestuous relationship. He was just a man doing what he thought was best at the time to keep his family together. His love for his family ran deeper than the Marianas trench and I respect him for that. I no longer hold bitterness toward this man and hope he is finding peace and happiness in the loving arms of God. He was a good man. I still do not agree with his approach, but lessons can be learned even in times of anguish and strife.

The lesson I learned is to never stand in the way of my children's decisions. If they seek my advice, I will give it to them with honesty, but I will never disown or stop loving them because they choose to ignore what I think is best for them. My children's lives are theirs to live. I know life can be unpredictable, burdensome, and sad, but I would only encourage them to strive to do their best at making the most of the time they have on earth.

I even discovered the cause of the putrid odor my son smelled in Indy. It was not emanating from my body, but it was emanating from my flip flops. The summer after drum corps, I put them on my feet and the foul odor nearly caused me to collapse. Unbeknownst to me, water had settled inside and become rancid. They are now safely and securely ensconced in the local landfill.

Oh, and as for Judyth, after an internal debate, I gave my *An Officer and A Gentleman* and *Jerry Maguire* combination movie script one more attempt. This time, it was successful. I drove to her place of employment, flowers in hand, and I greeted her inside her business. We went outside to her car and wept as we discussed our future. It turns out Judyth loved and missed me as much as I did her.

Judyth and I decided to give our relationship another try, and, since my initial writing, she moved in with me and we have become partners in this exciting yet challenging journey called life. We even went on a vacation to Italy, Turkey, and Greece together. It was a trip for the ages. We are making our own happy memories and I am back fighting for downtrodden clients, at least for a few more years when I hopefully retire.

In a little twist of good fortune, I found out that Alejandro Sanz, the Spanish musician who made me fall in love with Latin American and Spanish music and provided the soundtrack for my relationship with Judyth, was performing near Washington, DC. We attended the concert together. I sang as much as I could in Spanish, (which isn't much), and we built a memory that will last forever. I am pleased to say that I have devoted my life to this tremendous woman of faith and I am praying our relationship continues to flourish. I am still working on myself and rediscovering new thrills in the challenge of life, but so far, so good.

NOTES

3. THE GOOD OLD DAYS

1. Geoffrey Chaucer (1342-1400) - "The canterbury tales", from General Prologue, LL. 1-42. (n.d.). http://www.librarius.com/canttran/genpro/genpro001-042.htm

ABOUT THE AUTHOR

Robert L. Wegman was born in Ohio but grew up in rural North Carolina, where he spent many summers cropping tobacco and picking cucumbers under the scorching sun. As a young child, he developed a passion for music, particularly percussion, and eventually attended Atlantic Christian College (renamed Barton College) as a music education major. After completing his undergraduate studies, Mr. Wegman embarked on a career path as a music teacher, dedicating five and a half years to nurturing young talent and fostering their love for music.

In 1989, Mr. Wegman's journey took a turn toward more adventure when he applied for, and was commissioned as, an officer in the U.S. Coast Guard. After spending many years as a line officer, his leadership skills and commitment to service in the environmental response field led to his selection for the prestigious postgraduate legal program. He attended New York Law School, where he was nominated to be a member of the NYLS Law Review, and eventually graduated cum laude in 1996. After passing the New York and New Jersey bar exams, he became a Judge Advocate General (JAG) officer.

Mr. Wegman's legal acumen shone brightly as he navigated complex legal waters, including temporary assignments with the Navy JAG Corps and as a Special Assistant U.S. Attorney for the Department of Justice. His expertise was instrumental in both defending and prosecuting offenders in numerous court-martials, administrative separation boards, and civilian federal offenses.

In 2000, after rising to the rank of Lieutenant Commander, Mr. Wegman resigned his commission and transitioned to civilian life, joining the esteemed law firm of Paul, Hastings, Janofsky & Walker on Park Avenue in bustling Manhattan. There, he further honed his legal skills, delving further into environmental law, particularly for brownfield development projects.

Driven by a desire to make a more personal impact, Mr. Wegman returned to his legal roots in Virginia in 2003, where he established his own practice. Specializing in criminal and traffic defense, Mr. Wegman became a beacon of hope for those navigating the complexities of the legal system. With his unwavering commitment to his clients, his tenacious advocacy, and as a senior litigator, he has earned the respect and admiration of the legal community.

Throughout his varied career, Mr. Wegman has remained steadfast in his pursuit of justice, blending his passion for law with a deep-seated dedication to serving others. With each chapter, he continues to leave an indelible mark on the lives he touches, embodying the principles of integrity, compassion, and excellence.

This is Mr. Wegman's first attempt at writing a book about the recent tumultuous events that nearly ended his life. His sincere desire is that others will be encouraged to seek whatever help they need to thrive in an uncertain world.